QUEER EYE

Love Yourself. Love Your Life.

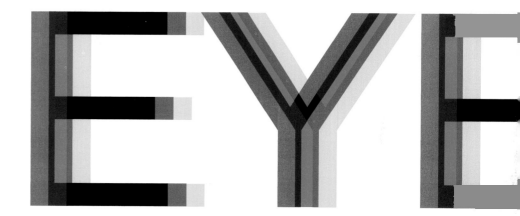

ANTONI POROWSKI,
TAN FRANCE,
JONATHAN VAN NESS,
BOBBY BERK &
KARAMO BROWN

WITH

MONICA CORCORAN HAREL

PHOTOGRAPHS BY
DENISE CREW & GAVIN BOND

ILLUSTRATIONS BY
PAIGE VICKERS

CLARKSON POTTER/PUBLISHERS
NEW YORK

*This book is 100 percent
dedicated to our fans.
We love you.*

CONTENTS

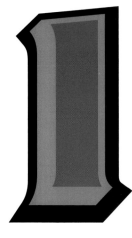

INTRODUCTION

Left to right: Executive producers Rob Eric, David Collins, and Michael Williams

*People always ask us, "How did it all begin?" Before we launch into that story, we should intro-*duce ourselves. We're David Collins, Michael Williams, and Rob Eric, the executive producers of *Queer Eye*, and we all work together with a gang of scruffy dogs in a little cottage-turned-office in Los Angeles. Our company is called Scout Productions. Yes, we're the guys who decided to reboot *Queer Eye for the Straight Guy*—which originally debuted more than fifteen years ago—and we couldn't be happier that you love it. (That seems like a safe assumption since you picked up this book.) If you watched the original series on Bravo, welcome back. If you're new to *Queer Eye* culture, let's take you back to the beginning.

The year was 2001. We—Michael and David—were living in Boston and producing independent movies together. One sunny afternoon in the fall, we were at an art gallery opening when we saw a woman berating her disheveled husband for his untucked shirt and messy hair. "Look at you. Why did you wear those socks? Why can't you dress more like them?" she said, pointing to a group of gay men drinking wine in the corner. She was so loud that everyone in the gallery heard her—and winced.

Without missing a beat, the guys rushed over to the poor husband's defense like knights in designer armor. "Ease up," they said to the woman. "Just give him a chance." They told the man to tuck in his shirt, fix his messy hair, and then said, "See? He's not that bad." In essence, they showed the wife that she married the right guy, but he just needed a little help and some kindness. Inspiration struck at that moment.

David looked at Michael and said, "Oh my God! Did you see that? That's our TV show."

"What show?" Michael asked.

David replied, "Queer eye for the straight guy!"

Eighteen months later, *Queer Eye for the Straight Guy* starring Carson Kressley, Thom Filicia, Ted Allen, Kyan Douglas, and Jai Rodriguez debuted on Bravo and became a huge breakout hit. A huge part of that success was thanks to another executive producer named David Metzler, the "Straight Guy" to David's "Queer Eye" on the show; Rob hadn't yet joined the team. (Fun fact: Rob actually auditioned to be the grooming expert on the original Queer Eye in 2002. At the time, he was roommates with Carson Kressley, who ultimately got the part of the style expert. Personally, we think Rob landed an even better role when he signed on to be part of Scout Productions.)

What a lot of people don't know is that the word "queer" was considered way too risqué for a TV show title in the early 2000s. In fact, in the state of New York—of all places!—it was illegal to even use "queer" in the name of a business. But we pushed for it anyway. We wanted to take back the word, which had become an insult, and make it our own.

Above: David, Karamo, and Tan in the field shooting.

Left, top to bottom: The moment after the show was nominated for an Emmy. Producers Rachelle Mendez, Rob Eric, David Collins, and Jen Lane are joined by Netflix executive Jenn Levy. Jen Lane and Rob Eric shooting season 2. Five of the executive producers immediately following the 2018 Emmy win; from left to right, Jen Lane, David Collins, Michael Williams, Rob Eric, and Rachelle Mendez.

Opposite: Scout Productions team, left to right, Trent Johnson, Michael Williams, David Collins and Coco, Joel Chiodi and Pickle, and Rob Eric and Tiberius.

Since then, the LGBTQ community has made incredible strides: We can get married; in most states, we have rights in the workplace; and "queer" is now a term of empowerment. It's a whole new cultural landscape. What better time to bring back *Queer Eye*.

But even more important, the show, at its core, was always about positivity and uniting people. With our country divided on so many issues, we imagined the modern version as even more of a bridge to bring people together. David kept saying, "People need a show right now that makes them feel good."

We also knew that our reboot would have to be as impactful as the original show. After lots of development meetings and countless take-out containers, we figured out how to finesse the formula. First of all, we took the Fab Five, who helped only men in the New York metropolitan area on the old show, to places where they would meet all types of people—especially our "heroes"—with completely different values. We wanted them to roll into towns where they stood out and won over locals by being themselves. Let's just say that you don't see a group of gay men on many street corners in the rural South—even in the tiny town of Gay, Georgia.

Left: *Queer Eye* creator and executive producer David Collins.

But in order to bring people together, you have to share your personal experiences. That's how we bond. On the original show, the guys didn't talk about coming out or discuss their boyfriends. (Back then, lots of gay people didn't feel safe talking openly about their personal lives either.) We like to say that the first Fab Five flew in like superheroes, saved the day, and flew out. Not anymore. This time around, you get to know the guys intimately. You learn that Bobby grew up as an evangelical Southern boy, while Tan, who is Middle Eastern, married a Mormon cowboy. We get to tell all of their fascinating stories, as they share their victories and their vulnerabilities. The result is a much deeper shared experience than any superhero moment.

Which brings us to how we found the new Fab Five. We knew we wanted a diverse cast that felt more representative of the world we live in. The search took months and we met thousands of experts in grooming, food and wine, style, culture, and home design. In the end, it was down to forty guys and casting felt a lot like speed dating. We realized that their chemistry was key to the success of the show so we played mix-and-match with different groups to see how they worked together as a team. What we didn't know was that Karamo, Tan, Bobby, Antoni, and Jonathan had already bonded. They were on a group text chain throughout the casting process.

Why those guys? Well, Karamo killed us with his confidence and his ability to get right to the interior of someone. Here was this single dad, handsome as hell, and so thoughtful. Tan epitomized our mantra of style, taste, and class even *before* he opened his mouth. Once we heard that charming accent and felt how sincere he was, we were sold. Bobby wowed us with his incredible talent as an interior designer, and we knew he would have the stamina to handle a huge project on every episode. We were aware of Jonathan's hilarious persona from his cult web series, *Gay of Thrones*, but we didn't come to know the depth of his innate kindness, smarts, and curiosity until later. He's a walking Wikipedia page! Plus, his unabashed sense of self and openness reminded us that everyone wants to be someone who can smile and say, "I am who I am, baby. Love it or leave it!"

Now, Antoni was originally part of another team of five when we were casting for chemistry, but the other four guys rallied for him like a brother. He had a passion for food that we just hadn't ever seen before. He genuinely wanted to teach the whole world how to cook.

Ultimately, we knew this Fab Five had enough heart to genuinely help people. And for the record, they don't get any information on our "heroes" before they meet them. That's a rule we never bend or break. On every episode, they blast into people's lives like tornadoes and build up their confidence through kindness, care, and humor. You see how that newfound confidence can completely change someone's life. For us, the payoff is that transformation and how it inspires a person to grow, take a chance, or face an emotional challenge.

We're pretty sure those breakthroughs have made you diehard fans, too.

The Fab Five hear from you all of the time through social media. But every day, we receive letters and emails from people—like you— who share how the show has changed their lives. Just knowing that *Queer Eye* not only entertains but has also become a force of good tells us that we're doing something right. We pass your letters around the office. We learn from them. So don't stop reaching out to us. Years ago, our little show started a conversation by introducing America to real gay men. With the new *Queer Eye*, the dialogue is now about finding common ground so we can all relate to each other better and respect our differences.

Right: Executive producers David Collins, Michael Williams, and Rob Eric.

Times sure have changed since the first *Queer Eye* debuted, but the core of what we believe remains the same. We don't do makeovers; we do make-betters. Ultimately, our heroes remind us that we're really not that different, right? We all laugh. We all cry. (Yes, even we producers still tear up when we watch an episode for the seventh time.) But mostly, at the end of the day, we all just want to be loved.

WELL, HELLO!

On *Queer Eye,* we literally barge into the lives of our "heroes" to learn all about them. Antoni wants to know exactly what they ate for breakfast. Jonathan runs his fingers through their hair. Karamo inevitably makes them cry—in a good way, of course. We do this because we know how important it is to make a deep and meaningful connection. We ask questions because we care. Our interaction with our heroes is fast and furious. But it's definitely not fleeting.

We stay in touch with all of them. Bobby gets texts in the middle of the night about where to move a sofa. Tan approves new slim-cut jeans via FaceTime. The point is that being on *Queer Eye* means making lasting relationships that transcend a TV show. When we signed up to be the new Fab Five, not one of us realized just how much of an impact we could make on people's lives. We weren't even certain that you, the fans, would let us into your homes—much less make this movement a cultural phenomenon.

But now we know. As Jonathan likes to say, "It's kind of like how Britney Spears felt after her first album." That means it's surreal but it also feels great. We're thrilled that people like you want more positivity and human connection in your lives. For us, *Queer Eye* is about the realization that we're all similar in so many ways, no matter where we live or what we wear or whom we choose to love.

We're just as surprised by how much we love each other, too! (Full disclosure: Tan had a thing for Karamo and Jonathan on the very first day we all met.) Our dynamic is always changing, but Karamo likes to describe us as a family: He's the hot dad (of course), Bobby is the get-it-all-done mom, Tan is the nice big brother, Antoni is the eager-to-please middle child, and Jonathan is the beautiful baby who brings us all so much joy.

At the end of the day, though, we know that connecting is all about quid pro quo. We have lives outside of *Queer Eye,* and we also have pretty fascinating backstories to share about the paths that led us to where we are today. Were we always this Fab? (Yes, but thanks for asking.) But who doesn't remember what we said as kids when we wanted to get to know each other: "You tell me your story, I'll tell you mine."

Living Out Loud with

JONATHAN
VAN NESS

ABOUT A BEAUTIFUL BOY

VITALS

Specialty Grooming

I'm an Aries. I think it's a fire sign and I'm fiery!

Fast Facts L.A. hairstylist and salon owner; creator of the wildly popular and Emmy-nominated Funny or Die web series, Gay of Thrones. Also, Jonathan hosts a weekly podcast called Getting Curious with guests like TV's W. Kamau Bell, Olympic skater Mirai Nagasu, and his mom.

What's most shocking about me? I can change a tire in five minutes, thanks to my stepdad.

My guilty pleasure movie The Cutting Edge. Who would have thought this retired hockey player who could not make the Olympic team would be the missing piece to a figure skater's Olympic dream?

I have always demanded to live out loud. Growing up in Quincy, Illinois, there was no one else marching to my particular drumbeat, though. The town had about forty thousand people. My immediate family owned the local TV station and newspaper, where I grew up running around journalists in newsrooms. I'm the youngest of three boys and the only one who didn't go into the business. My mom was always my best friend. As the daughter of the owner of the newspaper, she worked twice as hard as the other employees for half of the respect. She's so talented and so smart.

When I was in seventh grade, I started answering "Um, yes" to the question "Are you gay?" But I had known at age five that I was different. By the time those Bowflex commercials came around (I was about seven by then), I was like, "I am gay, for sure."

Of course, I stood out. I was obsessed with figure skating, the Spice Girls, gymnastics, and guinea pigs—oh, and Pop-Tarts! People knew me. I was really gregarious and flamboyant. My shine could not be dimmed. My middle brother, Tom, was six-two and the captain of the baseball team, so no one talked shit about me around him. My other brother played football. I was the school's first male cheerleader. Tom and I both got "Most School Spirit" at our high school.

But even though I was loud and boisterous, I was also really sensitive. I got picked on *a lot*. I was very insecure because I was bullied—even tormented—so much. I got my sense of humor from having to

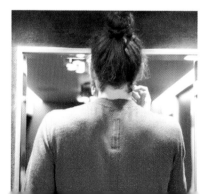

entertain myself when things got bad. And that trait has impacted me into my adult life. These experiences growing up turned me into an introverted extrovert: I do love who I am and I do love to entertain people, but I also need to spend time alone. I know—it's practically unbelievable that I like to be alone to recharge, but it's true.

The road to loving and accepting myself and becoming confident has been a long one for me, because it began in a place where I was so uncomfortable in my surroundings. Being who I am is a constant process, and every day I still work on that relationship with myself. I have definitely done affirmations in the mirror, telling myself "I'm enough." Yes, I am. That's probably why I focus so much on the inside—instead of just the outside—with my hair salon clients and the heroes on *Queer Eye*. I know that a few minutes of me time is so important for myself, too.

FOLLOWING MY HEART— AND MY HAIR

When I was four, I had a strict bedtime of eight o'clock. But the only time I was allowed to break that rule was on the nights of the Miss USA, Miss America, and Miss Universe pageants. My mom and I would watch together and make scorecards—especially about the hair. We loved to talk about how big the hair was in relation to the shoulder pads of the dress. That was when I started to notice how hair shapes the face and how hairstyles relate to silhouettes. And don't think I didn't take notes on men's grooming with that Regis Philbin onstage.

I was always a total beauty product person, too. My family went on a road trip to the Mall of America when I was eight, and we all got $100 to spend. I spent $98 of it at Bath & Body Works! My mom was so pissed off because she couldn't believe this saleswoman let an eight-year-old spend $98 by himself at Bath & Body Works. I got this fierce face peel, body scrub, and all the freesia body butter you could handle. I was obsessed with it.

When I was seventeen, I went to the University of Arizona for a semester with a partial cheerleading scholarship. But I dropped out because my passion was hair—and I knew college was not for me even

though I do love to learn. So I took out a loan and enrolled in the Aveda Institute in Minneapolis. At the time, it had the hardest cosmetology program in the country. I learned to do acrylic nails, pin curls, roller sets, facials—you name it, girl. One hair out of place and you failed!

After that, I moved back to Arizona and started doing hair in Scottsdale. I had my own clientele and everything, but I knew I needed more experience in order to grow. What I was missing was that *Devil Wears Prada* experience—a boot camp. I knew how not to mess up a simple cut and color, but I didn't know how to fix anything that might land in my chair. If you came in and said, "I want a white-blond bob to my chin," first of all, I didn't know how to talk you out of it. And second of all, even if I thought it was a good idea, I didn't know how the hell to do it! I needed to be working around people who could talk to their clients and say, "This just isn't achievable for you, honey"—and be confident in saying that.

So I packed up, moved to Los Angeles in 2009, and went to work at Sally Hershberger. I like to say that I learned how to cut myself out of a paper bag there, because it was such a great education in how to do hair. But it was really, really stressful. The Devil was indeed wearing Prada, honey. A stylist once threw a pair of scissors at me! I cried every day for a year and a half. I made something like $8 an hour and got bad tips. To support myself, every weekend I would drive six hours to Arizona with my own color and do twenty of my clients in two days. (Um, it was a lot. About eight clients a day would be a normal amount of work.) After a year and a half, I was done with all that craziness. I was ready to be on my own.

But then, everything went dark. My stepfather—I called him my dad—got sick with bladder cancer, so I went home to Illinois to be closer to him for what would end up being six months. He came into my life when I was just six and he was this amazing person, the glue of my family. He took on the role of stay-at-home dad while my mom worked at the paper. Watching someone die of cancer is an awful process, and it took its toll on me, too. I gained seventy pounds in three months. One night, I ordered $29 worth of Taco Bell—that did not even include a drink, honey—and ate it all. Do I still self-soothe with food? Always. As a kid, I loved powdered sugar donuts, and I loved Tower Pizza in my hometown, which has this gorgeous white cheese dip. This talk is making me hungry. The older I get, though, the more I am all about balance.

It took me almost two years to lose the weight I gained after my dad died in 2012. I did it by getting back to my yoga practice when I returned to L.A. (I had fallen in love with yoga when I was nineteen.) I was militant about it. Then, I got certified as a yoga teacher so I could strengthen my practice, and I taught for a while, too. There was a time when I was like, "Oh my God, I have to lose this weight because if I don't, then who's going to date

me?" You probably noticed that I'm the only single one on the show. Sometimes it's more fun because I'm totally independent, sometimes it's not. Do I want to be in a gorgeous relationship with someone I'm in love with? Yes! I just haven't met him yet.

But now my working out is all about me. I go to the gym every day. I'm finding my happy place because I don't have a crazy Adonis-like body and that's fine. I just want to be fit and have good blood pressure and feel good with my clothes off—and I do. I love my body, but I think that there's always a part of me that wishes I looked more like Antoni. Or like an underwear model. But then again I still really love to binge-eat McDonald's at night so . . .

Okay, wait, so back to my career. I moved back to L.A. in my early twenties and started rebuilding my clientele by working at a salon in Venice, by the beach. A few years later, I opened my own little hair salon in L.A. with a partner. It has three chairs, one shampoo bowl, and it's super-cute and intimate. No bad energy, I promise!

Every month, I do hair for just one day, because of my busy schedule, and see a bunch of my clients. One after another. Can you believe? But I love going back because doing hair is everything to me. It's what I love to do.

I DON'T CARE . . . BUT I REALLY, REALLY DO

When I first read that Queer Eye *was being rebooted, I espe-*cially loved the idea of turning red states pink—that's what the producers said they were setting out to do—one makeover at a time. Or just connecting with people who don't look like me or think like me. I'm really compassionate and I don't even know why. Maybe it's because I come from a place where there are a lot of conservatives, so I know that plenty of conservatives are still good people.

When I had my first audition meeting, I was just like, "You're not going to get this, girl." I looked super-haggard that day because I'd been running around doing hair

"Being who I am is a constant process, and every day I still work on my relationship with myself."

appointments. My own long hair was a mess; I had scruff on my face. I thought, "They're going to want someone who actually looks like a groomer, duh." Someone gorge like Tan with his literally perfect hair. But I was so inspired by the original *Queer Eye*. I was such a fan of it in junior high and high school, and like, I just wanted it so bad. I wanted it to be truly representative, too.

So what I said at that audition was "I don't care if I get a callback"—even though I was lying and I really, really did!—"but I hope you cast a diverse cast. It needs to be diverse." I think in that moment, the casting directors realized just how much I cared about the show and how it would be viewed and its impact and they said to me in the room, "Okay. You can come back." And I did. And you know what happened next, honey.

Being on *Queer Eye* has taught me not to get too attached to the success. I'm excited by it, and it's amazing, but I don't want to *need* it. I just want to work hard and be passionate about whatever I'm doing. I try really hard not to compare myself to anyone else. I've learned from my yoga practice and teaching yoga that comparison is the thief of all joy. When I hear that competitive voice, I'm like, "I totally understand why you would feel like that, but I need you to calm down, girl. There's totally enough success for everyone." I'm really into the law of abundance versus the law of scarcity. So deep, right?

THE THING ABOUT GETTING GORGE

When I talk about my idea of grooming for Queer Eye, *I really* want to break down that concept of a metrosexual. There was this whole movement in the early 2000s of what it meant to be a man getting a spray tan and a faux hawk and popping his collar. I'm more about self-care and bringing a perspective of overall well-being to people. For me, like I said, it's an inside and an outside job. I just want to help you look and feel great.

That doesn't mean looking perfect, though. I'm cool with imperfection and having messy hair, because the same goes for life. I think I made peace a long time ago with the fact that I won't ever be perfect. I also wanted what I didn't have for, like, forever. That's part of the human condition. As a kid, all I wanted was long hair, but I wasn't allowed to grow it out. Look at me now making up for it by tossing my mane left and right! Letting people see *you* is beautiful. But if you're that person who doesn't leave the house without being fully done up and you're just serving face all day because that's what makes you feel great, I love that, too.

From JVG's personal photo collection

JUST A SMALL-TOWN BOY

Some people know at an early age exactly what they want to do and who they want to be. That's just not my story. Where I grew up, in Miller, Missouri, home design wasn't a thing. The only time I ever saw an interior designer was on a TV show about sassy decorators living in Atlanta called *Designing Women*. And all of that happened in a big, faraway city, as far as I knew. But there was something innate in me—I would rearrange my parents' bedroom and living room furniture while they were at work. And I redid my room all by myself with a dinosaur theme when I was five years old. The color scheme was blue, green, and yellow—and all *very* put together, thank you very much.

No one ever really saw my chic take on interiors, mind you. When people talk about being from a small farm town, I laugh and bet them mine was smaller. Imagine living in a farmhouse with only two neighbors within a mile in any direction. My Christian school was just one big room from first grade to twelfth, and we all sat at cubicle-style desks facing the wall. We just made our way through workbooks at our own pace. You didn't talk at all. When you had a question, you raised a little American flag instead of raising your hand. A parent volunteer came over to help. There was no teacher. Weird, right? No wonder I was awkward as a child. I wasn't allowed to watch TV or listen to the radio at home, either. Even today, when I'm in a room full of people I don't know, I sort of regress to that quiet, shy boy. People assume I'm being reserved or snobby, but nope. It's because I grew up surrounded by more cows than kids.

love the one-liners, which I still use, and just the way that they looked for the good in everyone.

Biggest pet peeve? Self-absorbed people who are not aware of anyone around them. They leave a cart in the middle of an aisle at a store or double park and block the road. Ugh.

Who am I in three words? Hardworking. Determined. Ambitious.

My life to-do list starts with learn Vietnamese. I can speak it a little, especially when I'm around my husband's relatives.

Where will I be in ten years? Hopefully, running a little boutique hotel on the beach in Vietnam, where my husband, Dewey, is from originally. I love the country, the people, the food.

But I wasn't just awkward; I stood out. The old farmers would look at me and say, "You don't belong here, boy. You belong in New York City." I thought, "Yeah, tell me something I don't know." Beginning when I was eight, I definitely had a sense that I was meant to do bigger things—or to be someone with a higher purpose than staying in my hometown. But I didn't even know where to begin. It didn't help that I was fifteen and my mother still made me go to bed at eight-thirty every night! She and my father were protective—and very, very religious. And of course, I couldn't come out or even talk to anyone about being gay in my dusty little cow town. The one guy I'd ever known to come out was almost killed when some jerks ran him off the road one night. But I had to do something. I was wearing a mask every day, and the anger it was bringing me was building up. I had to get out of there.

Finally, I hit my breaking point. I couldn't handle the oppression anymore. My parents always used this phrase to threaten me and my sister during an argument—"If you don't like the rules, there's the door." One night after we butted heads, I walked through that door. I had just had enough. I only moved about thirty miles away, to Springfield, aka "Queen City of the Ozarks," but it was a huge leap for me at fifteen.

AN EPIPHANY IN A 1984 BUICK

When I got to Springfield, I had absolutely nothing to my name. I stayed on friends' crummy sofas; sometimes I lived on the streets. I was terrified, but I knew I had taken the first step on my way to somewhere. Obviously, the first thing I needed was a place to live. I found an apartment that cost $425 a month, and I needed three roommates to swing it. To get by, I worked a bunch of different jobs: sales clerk at the Gap and the Body Shop and, wait for it, graveyard shift attendant at a gas station. Oh, and it gets worse. That gas station got robbed all the time when I was working. But hey, when you're making minimum wage in Missouri, which at the time was $5.14 an hour, you have to really work it.

And it's not like I could save money, either. It didn't feel like I was making a living; it felt like I was living a nightmare. It was better than being pent up in my parents' house, but man, it was tough. Then one

Young Bobby getting an early start to his career.

day, my friend and I were driving to work and the street we normally took was closed, so I detoured through a parking lot. But every exit in the lot was blocked off, too. Grrr. I was stuck in a freaking parking lot with nowhere to go. Talk about a sign! I screeched my crappy Buick to a halt and slammed the steering wheel. "This is how I feel in Missouri!" I shouted. "Every exit is blocked. I'm not doing anything with my life!"

Within literally twenty-four hours, I was on my way to Denver in a U-Haul with my car attached on a trailer. (That damn car broke down two days later—probably another sign—but I was out.) I picked Denver because I had only one friend outside of Missouri, whom I had met online, and that's where he lived. He had actually helped me deal with the fact that I was gay and guided me on coming out. My boss at the Body Shop lined me up with a job as a manager at the Body Shop near the Denver airport. But when I first drove into the deep valley surrounded by mountains, I saw the massive city below and

totally freaked out. I pulled over and started crying. "Oh my God! I've made a huge mistake," I thought. "I'm never going to survive here." Fear can motivate you if you channel it right. I knew if I didn't make a quick, drastic change and act on that desperate feeling of being trapped—the feeling I'd had since my childhood—I'd be right back to that daily grind of working three jobs and I'd be there forever. I got a gig working at a high-end national furnishings store called the Bombay Company, which (perhaps unintentionally) stoked that interest I'd had in interior design as a kid. But within a few years, I had grown out of Denver and set my sights on a new frontier.

In 2003, I moved to New York City with $100 in my pocket and one suitcase. Who does that?! Me, again. It was June 23, and the Gay Pride Parade was snaking its way through Chelsea, where I had prepaid three months' rent on a two-bedroom apartment. I was walking around my new neighborhood and looking at all of these crazy floats and flamboyant, free people marching around. It was beautiful, but it was too much for little old me. I was still a repressed farm boy at heart. "Oh my God! I'm never going to make it here," I thought again.

GETTING FIRED, GETTING FIRED UP

Boy, was I wrong that time. Within a month, this kid from Podunk, Missouri, had fast-talked his way into a job as manager of Restoration Hardware in SoHo. I saw the appeal of sumptuous bedding and thick, plush towels and was able to make a job of it. There, I came to appreciate how home design impacts people's lives. One night, my team and I were working late to get the store ready because a TV show was coming to shoot there. Yes, it was *Queer Eye for the Straight Guy*! We worked until 2 a.m. to make it perfect, and perfect it was. We were so exhausted from working so hard that we all forgot to punch out—that's a big deal when you're working an hourly job. The next morning, the general manager took it upon herself to clock us all out at 8 p.m. When I noticed the error, I fixed my own time and my team's time, too. It was totally against the rules to adjust your punch-out time, and no mercy was shown. I was fired. I kid you not.

I bounced back quickly with a job at Portico, another upscale design store, but eventually I also got let go from there when the company went bankrupt. Come to think of it, I've been fired from every job I've ever had! So what do you do then? I knew I had to work for myself. One guy who canned me said, "You're never going to amount to anything." Clearly, he wasn't psychic. But along the way, I must have had some grand plan, even though I probably didn't know it at the time. I was a total sponge at every job I ever worked, learning everything and anything I could about the home goods business. I studied why people bought certain furniture. I watched how design trends affected the market. And I even taught myself how to build an e-commerce site.

When I was twenty-six, I opened my first Bobby Berk Home store in SoHo. This is a long, crazy story, but in order to do that, I had to take on a partner and his $600,000 in debt. My friends who worked on Wall Street thought I had lost it. "You're insane, Bobby. Why on earth would you do that?" Um, it's called taking a leap of faith, people. Less than a year after that, I paid it all off and bought out my partner. I'm proud to say that I have never had an investor or taken out a loan in my life. Within ten years, I opened stores in Miami, Los Angeles, and Atlanta, too.

Having those stores taught me how much I love the design process. Nothing makes me happier than when people I have worked with on their spaces tell me they can't wait to get home simply because they enjoy being there. In 2016, I launched Bobby Berk Interiors + Design so I could work even more closely with private clients.

I don't usually get into all the tragic details of my career path because for a long time, I was very ashamed about dropping out of high school and not having studied design formally. I usually gloss over all that when I talk to anyone about my past. But now I think my true story needs to be told. Who knows? If I had taken a more linear path and gone back to school, I might not be where I am now. My career trajectory shows that anybody can break out and shine, especially young gay people who have been kicked out of their home and don't know what they're going to do with their lives. But just to be clear, I'm not necessarily suggesting that *you* skip school and run to Manhattan. Working so many different jobs, I learned how to hustle. I learned how to fake it when I didn't know something, until I finally did.

"Working so many different jobs,
I learned how to hustle. I learned
how to fake it when I didn't know
something, until I finally did."

A FRESH TAKE ON FAMILY

Outside of work, I cultivated a whole new circle of friends, too. People say that you can't choose your family, but that's not the case in my book. In the gay community, we literally use the phrase "chosen family." Even if it's not who you expected, there will be people there for you who love you unconditionally. They're always out there. So many friends helped me get to where I am today.

In 2004, I met my surgeon husband Dewey, online, and we've been together ever since. He's one of the kindest and genuinely sweetest people. When Dewey and I are together, we are always right next to each other. We're not traditionally romantic, but we are affectionate. He's calmed me down and I've brought him out of his shell. In the beginning, he was so soft-spoken and never raised his voice. Most of my friends actually thought he was snobby, but I told them he was just terribly shy. Now when we have an argument, which is rare, he'll be the one yelling and I'm like, "What? Why are you raising your voice?"

A lot of people, like me, get rejected by their parents and siblings when they come out. I never even told my family I was gay; someone outed me to them after I left home. And as you can imagine, they definitely didn't have very nice things to say to me. I wasn't surprised by their words, but that didn't make them hurt any less. But know that people from whom you're estranged might come back into your life. Fast-forward to two or three years later, and my parents contacted me and said, "We're sorry for how we treated you." We've been totally good ever since—we're actually really close now. I recently bought my mom a car, and one for my dad, too. But what's funny is that I never really splurge on

myself. Coming from such a poor background and being so broke for a lot of my adult life, I still have a really hard time spending money on myself. But it felt great to do something nice for them.

Being on *Queer Eye* has expanded that chosen family in unexpected ways as well. When I first heard about the reboot, I knew I wanted to be part of it. The original was a groundbreaking show and it meant so much to me—even if it did get me fired! I remember watching it every week at my friend's apartment in New York. You had these five guys who were so proud and happy, with great careers. At the audition, I bonded right away with Jonathan, Antoni, Karamo, and Tan; we had instant chemistry. But I didn't realize then that I was gaining four new brothers. Do we drive each other crazy sometimes?

Of course, but we love each other anyway—that's what family is.

One day driving back from a shoot, we were all in the car and playing this random game we call "real *Walking Dead*." You have to decide who will be the first to die if there's a zombie apocalypse. Jonathan suddenly says, "Definitely Bobby," and I'm like, "What do you mean? I'm a survivor. I lived on the streets!" He responded, "You'd be making sure everyone else would be getting out safely and then you'd definitely get eaten." He's probably right. And sometimes family knows you better than you know yourself.

DO IT ANYWAY

I always say I don't have any regrets. That doesn't mean I think I'm perfect or I haven't made mistakes. There are a lot of things I had to do that will not be in this book—or *any* book ever—that make me look back and think, "How the hell am I still alive?" But still, I don't regret anything. If I hadn't learned those lessons of being scrappy and struggling when I was younger, I easily could have screwed everything up when I was older.

My advice to anyone with a dream is pretty simple: just keep pushing. When people tell you to follow the rules or that you can't or shouldn't try something new, do it anyway. Trust your passion. I can't tell you how many times someone (including me) said, "Bobby, that will never work." When people ask me how to decorate a living room or which dining room table to buy, I tell them, "Focus on what makes *you* happy. Don't focus on what's hot right now."

That applies to life, though. Trust your gut in your home, at your job, and in your relationships. I'm so glad I took chances, even though I was afraid. It would've taken me decades to accomplish what I have done if I hadn't pushed through my fear. More than once in my career, I have thought, "Wow, I'm taking a huge risk and it might destroy me." And most of those risks paid off. Remember that kid who never thought he would survive in Denver or New York? I guess if my life were a movie, this is the point where I would shout: "Oh my God! I can make it anywhere." Roll credits.

From Bobby's personal photo collection

TAN FRANCE

Doesn't Care About Trends

the more technical route and learn how to design apparel instead of couture. The former is for the clothing racks; the latter is for the red carpet. If I was going to follow my dream, I still wanted to be practical. After I finished school, I worked for Zara corporately so I could learn about retail operations, and then I went to work as the menswear department manager at Selfridges in London to learn how department stores choose their inventory. If a high-profile client came in, I would go down to the floor and work as a stylist with him. God, I sound so corporate! My idea was to learn enough to be an entrepreneur one day.

Working in fashion, I felt like I had to move to New York. So I did when I was twenty-three, but I only spent three and a half months living there before a friend from Salt Lake City convinced me to visit his home with him. I fell in love with that city! People are amazed when I tell them that, but to me, Utah was stunning. I had never even seen mountains before. Everyone was so friendly and wanted to get to know me, even if it was in passing. The city reminded me of a little village. I was in complete awe of New York, and I never wanted to go to sleep because I was afraid I would miss something there, but Salt Lake City felt more like a place I could live forever. I turned to my friend and said, "One day I want to make this my home."

About two years later, I did move there, but I still found a way to follow my dream. I worked for more fash-

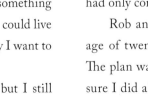

ion companies in Salt Lake City, such as Shade Clothing, so I could learn about manufacturing and the wholesale business. In 2016, I launched my first women's contemporary line, called the Rachel Parcell Collection, with a local fashion blogger. I was terrified because I had put every penny I owned into it. Then, another line, called Kingdom & State, followed a year later. I went on to acquire two more fashion companies, so I had four in total at one time.

TWO MEN AND A LOT OF BABIES

It wasn't all work, though. I met my now-husband Rob online in 2008, shortly after I had moved. He's a cowboy from Wyoming who was raised Mormon, so even though we had different backgrounds, we had things in common right from the get-go, as neither of us drinks or smokes. Plus, I thought he was very, very hot. Our first date lasted four hours. We went to lunch and then we went to coffee somewhere else because we wanted to keep talking. When I first met the man who would become my father-in-law, he had never met a person of color, or a gay person other than his son, who had only come out a couple of weeks before.

Rob and I will be dads one day, for sure. From the age of twenty-five, I have wanted children desperately. The plan was always for me to work my arse off to make sure I did all I could to build up a few businesses. Then, once I started a family with Rob, I would sell them for

a major profit so I could stay at home and raise the kids. And I knew I needed to create a few businesses, because ideally, I want a minimum of four children—preferably six. Yes, a lot! And all of that was going according to plan until I got the call from a casting director about the new *Queer Eye* . . .

SERIOUSLY, I WILL RUIN YOUR SHOW

Initially, I said, "No, thanks." I was a business owner determined to retire early in life—and at that point, I had sold three out of four of my companies. I had almost made it! I had never been a TV person, and auditioning at all seemed like a waste of time because I knew for a fact they would never cast me. I never even had my picture taken when I was growing up, because we didn't do that in my religion. So the idea of being in front of a camera made me very nervous. Having said that, the idea of representing Middle

Eastern people on TV *did* intrigue me. Seeing yourself on TV or in movies is so important, and we don't give the entertainment industry enough credit for how exposure of a culture, or lack thereof, can affect a community's mentality. Everyone's mentality, really. I wish I could have seen a gay Middle Eastern on TV when I was a kid! That would have shown me I could achieve anything and be anyone, whereas in reality, all I ever thought I wanted to be was white because I thought that was the only way you could get on in this world. So I agreed to fly to L.A. for three days of auditions.

On the first day, I was quieter than everyone else because I was so nervous. The other people there were very "showbiz." I didn't know how to do that, how to act; I only knew how to be myself. At one point, one of the producers said, "Can you turn it up? Can you give us more American?" American TV and British TV are very different; we don't get that animated. So I just said, "Nope. I really can't. I'm not American." I was so convinced I

"I created this path entirely on my own. And I got here because I was really strong-willed and sometimes unruly—and I pushed for a life that wasn't meant to be mine."

would be cut that I had already planned where I would step out for brunch (a place I had read about called The Butcher, The Baker, The Cappuccino Maker) and go shopping (at this cool boutique called the Kooples). But, obviously, they never did cut me. In fact, the executive producer David Collins rang me that second morning to

say, "Just keep being yourself, Tan, and you will get the job." That was exactly the advice I needed to hear, but I still wasn't convinced.

When they next called, to tell me I got the job, five days after I came back to Salt Lake City, the first thing I said was "You're out of your mind! Give it to that other guy. I'm going to ruin your show." Of course by then I wanted it, though. I know it sounds silly, but I felt like I had already made some new best friends. There were about forty other guys on the first day. I met Karamo and Bobby immediately and we started chatting. I lent Karamo my big coat to wear as a blanket because he's always cold. On the next day, we got to know Jonathan. We met Antoni on the last day. Even before the audition process was done, Bobby created a group text called Fab Five. Of course that was presumptuous, but we all promised each other that if we didn't get the call, we would stay in touch because we got on great as mates. I really believe we would have, but of course we didn't have to find out. In that month and a half before we started working on the show, we texted each other a lot. Sometimes, fifty or sixty times a day!

COMING FULL CIRCLE

Well, I will say I was right about how much people appreciate seeing us on TV. People send me messages all the time, saying, "You just don't know what you've done for us." Some come up to me in public and say, "It's amazing that you're on TV." I represent a certain community that is usually struggling to just be themselves in real life. I understand that feeling. When I was younger, I definitely didn't have any confidence. If you were to ask my teachers in Doncaster, they would tell you I was the quietest boy in school. But I hit a point in my early twenties when I was no longer ashamed of my skin color and my heritage. I think it was in New York and Utah, where my heritage and look were a conversation starter. My complexion was no longer a hindrance in my life. It was something to be celebrated. That interest and acceptance gave me this new-found confidence and made me realize that what I represent is absolutely wonderful.

That confidence helped me believe I could achieve anything. Everything I have now never seemed like an option or a possibility for me before, considering where I come from. I created this path entirely on my own. And I got here because I was really strong-willed and sometimes unruly—and I pushed for a life that wasn't "meant" to be mine.

When I work with our heroes on the show now, they remind me of the time when I first started to experiment with clothes. Just being able to put forth who you really are, or who you really want to be, through your appearance, your first impression, is so important. You come into your own and start to feel like an individual. Maybe someone tries on clothes that actually fit for the first time or puts together pieces he or she never would have worn before. Seeing the amazed look on a face and watching that person stand differently or smile bigger into the mirror—it's really special. And who knows? Maybe I'll help that special somebody get lucky, too.

ANTONI POROWSKI

Doesn't Follow Recipes

MORE IS
MORE

No one is allowed to help me in my tiny Brooklyn kitchen when I'm cooking.
Whether I'm preparing something for a dinner party or just riffing on
a recipe for a casual supper, it's all me. Nobody chops. Nobody cooks.
Nobody cleans up. It's not that I'm controlling or that I want all of the
glory. (Okay, I may be a little picky.) I just go into full cook, waiter,
busboy, sommelier mode. I have to do it all because I want my guests to
have the ultimate experience.

Maybe I inherited that nature from my mother, who was born
in Warsaw and immigrated to Canada. My Polish father came from
Brussels. When I was a kid in Montreal, she would prepare these really
lavish meals for dozens of friends and family. She usually insisted on
doing everything herself. Neither my two sisters nor I were allowed to
help her in the kitchen, but I always watched. Once everything was ready
but before everyone arrived, my mother and father would have a cocktail
together and listen to Edith Piaf's "La Vie en Rose."

It sounds storybook romantic, I know, but my family was actually
pretty dysfunctional—loud with a lot of conflict and high tension. We
didn't talk about our deeper feelings at all; you kept everything stifled
inside. Food always connected us, though, no matter what. Every morning, we had the quintessential European breakfast: an array of fruit,
full charcuterie, cheeses, spreads, and fresh-baked breads. As Poles, we
also kept a lot of food in the house, maybe subconsciously because food
rations had been so sparse for my grandparents, who had survived a

Specialty Food & Wine

I'm a Pisces. It's a water
sign and I swam a lot as a
kid. Also, I'm intuitive and
artistic and very sensitive.

Fast Facts A New York-based
former model and actor, and
the co-owner of newly opened
eatery the Village Den,
Canadian Antoni lives in
Brooklyn with his boyfriend.

Most shocking about me?
I can ride a horse, change
its saddle, and groom it
like a pro.

My guilty pleasure movie is
<u>Cruel Intentions</u>. I wanted
to be Sebastian Valmont
growing up. I would whisper
the words as it was
playing—to the dismay of
anyone who was watching it
with me.

concentration camp during the Holocaust, where they had been placed even though they were Catholic. We had an extra fridge in the garage and two extra freezers in the basement.

And as you can imagine, holidays were a big deal. For Christmas Eve, we laid out a beautiful hand-embroidered tablecloth and kept fresh hay under the dining room table to represent the manger. There was always an extra seat at our table in case anyone unexpectedly stopped by. We ate pickled herring served two or three ways—my favorite was with sour cream and finely chopped apples—vegan borscht, this creamy potato salad, and little mushroom-filled dumplings called *uszka*. I recently spent Christmas with my sister in Ottawa and realized how much I miss those traditions. They remind me of my heritage, who I am and where I come from. If I have children, I will most definitely pass them on. I don't speak Polish as well as I did as a kid, but I can still do a great Polish accent.

LATE TO THE GAME

Even though in my family we kept the lid on our emotions, I'm probably more repressed than I even know. When I was growing up, sexuality felt extreme. You were either gay or straight. But being straight or gay was never a big part of my identity. That's not how I express myself.

But coming out wasn't traumatic for me, like it was for so many people. If I'd had a best friend like Jonathan—who's so strong and free in his sexuality—when I was growing up, maybe my preferences would have been different? Maybe I would have been open to dating guys and felt free? But back then, there wasn't as much fluidity as there is now. And for me, it's still shifting. I've had more lasting relationships with women than I've had with men. I actually dated a guy for a while when I was in my early twenties, and then went back to seeing women for several years. Now I'm in a relationship with a creative director, and we've been together since 2011.

When I told my father about my relationship, it was more about who I was spending time with than about labeling my sexual identity. He was driving me to the airport and commented that I was secretive about my

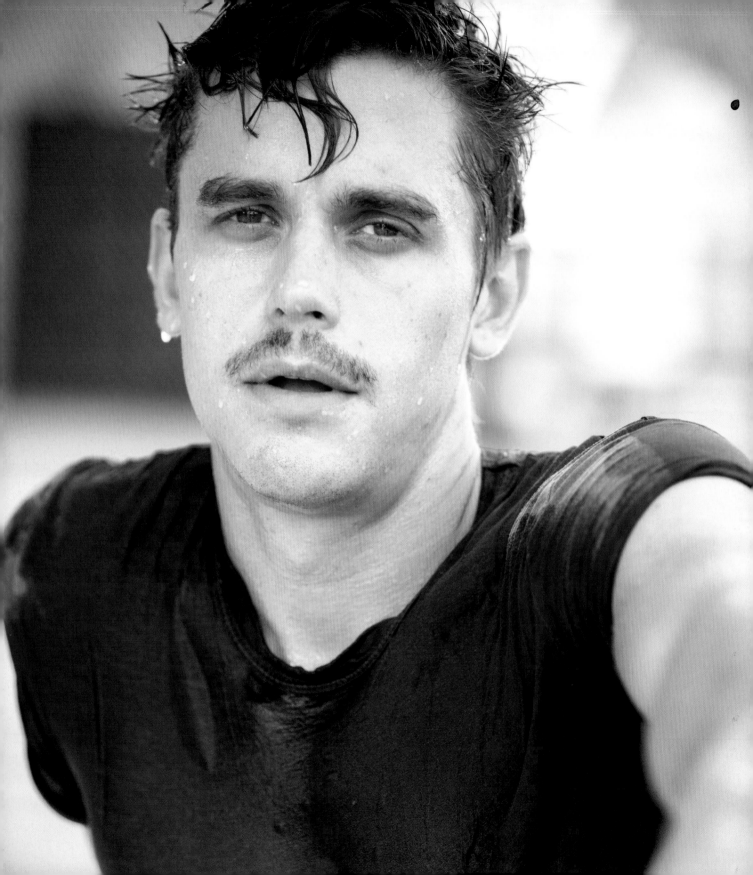

Young Antoni beginning his culinary career with his two sisters.

life. It was funny for my father to say that because he would never pry, but I think maybe he was finally trying to come into my life on a more personal level. His way of dealing with things is very gentle and slow instead of direct and blunt. Like I said, I didn't grow up in a household where you talked about your relationships—my sisters certainly never brought their boyfriends home.

I didn't say much in the car, but when the plane was taxiing on the runway, I thought, "If this plane crashes, I'm going to die and he's never going to know." Morbid, but motivating. So I decided to send my father an email. I wrote this: "I just want you to know that I love a man. I am loved. And we live together." He didn't respond at all. I have to admit it was kind of killing me not to hear anything back. But a week later, we were casually talking and I asked him if he got my email. My father said, "I would love to meet him." Like, that was it. The rest of my family reacted the same way when I mentioned that I was dating a man.

A ZIG HERE,
A ZAG THERE

My family always says I never shut up when I talked about food growing up. I would go on and on, describing the taste, the texture. Even though it's always been a passion of mine, I would never refer to myself as a chef. I didn't study at a culinary school or cook professionally. I guess you could say that a series of events led me to where I am now—nothing has really gone according to my master plan.

My first job ever was as a busboy at a family-run Polish restaurant in Montreal where grandmas were making pierogis in the basement. When I was in my teens, we moved to West Virginia, where my popularity plummeted. I was seen as the weird immigrant kid because I had an odd name, spoke a foreign language, and always brought these weird lunches like stuffed cabbage or vegetarian sandwiches on spelt bread to school.

I was ready to return to the city. So for college, I went back to Canada to study psychology. I loved to analyze how we think and behave. But really early on, I also knew I wanted to be an actor. There are a lot of doctors and engineers in my family, so I've always felt a bit like a black sheep in that respect. I remember when I watched *Cinema Paradiso* as a little kid. I just sat there, transfixed by everything on the screen. What a film. It was the only time I ever saw my father cry. (That is, until he watched an episode of *Queer Eye* with me . . . and wept.)

My passion for acting wasn't just about me wanting to be the next James Dean or River Phoenix. (Then again, what young actor doesn't?) I love everything about film, from the musical scores to the wardrobes to the set design. That part of me, now that I think about it, probably saw and loved all the drama that goes on in the restaurant world as well. You build this magical setting, you learn your lines, you put on a show. In the end, you create an experience for the audience.

After college, I moved to New York in 2009 to study acting at a conservatory and did what struggling artists do: I worked at restaurants. I've had every job there is in a restaurant, except being a chef. Eventually, in between auditions, I became the manager of a very hip, upscale Japanese restaurant in SoHo called Bond Street. The menu was very intimidating, but what I did there was teach the staff how to talk about the food in a way that made it really accessible and seductive. I told them to describe the dishes in terms that people could understand, like crunch and creaminess and how they harmonized together.

One night, my friend convinced me to go to hear the food and wine guy on *Queer Eye for the Straight Guy*, Ted Allen, read from his new book in Brooklyn. At the time, Ted Allen was the host of *Chopped*. I talked to him afterward, and we realized that we lived right across the street from each other. We became friends, and eventually I went to work for him and his husband as an assistant and pseudo personal chef. Not only did I learn culinary tips and shortcuts from Ted's famous chef friends, but I also had a huge kitchen (the size of my apartment, in fact) to use as a sort of science lab where I could invent flavors and craft recipes.

A QUEER EYE COINCIDENCE

So that Ted Allen guy? When I heard that *Queer Eye* was being rebooted, I asked him if he thought I had a shot and he helped me get an audition. And the rest is herstory, as Jonathan says.

It's a dream job. On the show, I get to do what I love: run into strangers' kitchens, look through their refrigerators and pantries, and smell (and often taste) their leftovers. Then we connect over food—and I help our heroes bring that connection into their lives. It's the same for me. Whether I'm cooking for close loved ones or someone I'm meeting for the first time and trying to impress, I get lost

"I guess you could say that a series of events led me to where I am now—nothing has really gone according to my master plan."

3^{FT} 6^{IN} NO DIVING

in the process and forget to be self-conscious. When I'm cooking, I don't care if I look cool or sound intellectual—and that's a great way for me to relax about how I'm being perceived. Because yes, I care way too much about what people think about me.

That's not a new thing for me. In my twenties, I had zero confidence. I wasn't comfortable in my own skin, and I made up for it by being overly charismatic. It got even crazier when I drank too much black coffee. I still go to that default occasionally, but now I'm comfortable with who I am and I feel like I am exactly where I need to be. On *Queer Eye*, we bring out the parts of people they want to work on and accentuate what's already there. A lot of our heroes are people pleasers. Being around those types of personalities forces me to be more introspective, too. One thing I have realized lately, especially in doing interviews and press, is that it is literally impossible to

make everybody happy. You can't do it. No matter how hard you try, you're always going to piss someone off. You're always going to be too good or not good enough in somebody's eyes. You have to accept that and just focus on the next step.

THE JOY OF COOKING

Some people think cooking is about rules. I'm not one of them. Baking is pretty scientific and you can't improvise too much, so I follow those recipes about 95 percent (I usually cut out a little bit of the sugar). But when I cook savory food, I never follow a recipe exactly. I skim the elements and figure out what I might want to add or substitute. I can't help myself. I'm always thinking about what I want every bite to include: A little acid? Richness? Some nuttiness?

Is that a metaphor for my life? I'm not sure. But I think there's a lot to be said for experimenting and being open to anything. Someone might tell you to follow a certain path, or a recipe for life—and maybe that will work for you. I used to think that you had to have a set thing, a defined aspiration that you're always working toward. But now, when people ask me what's next, I usually say, "We'll see." Not because I don't have strong ambitions—I do. I just have learned that you can't control everything in your life. It really comes down to faith. Just have faith in whatever you do—and whatever you cook.

From Antoni's personal photo collection

KARAMO BROWN

Chases Down His Dreams

UM, WE NEED TO TALK

VITALS

Specialty Culture

I'm a Scorpio, but I have no idea what that means.

Fast Facts Dad to Jason, twenty-one—whom he gained full custody of when he was nine; Karamo also adopted Jason's half-brother, Christian, now eighteen, two years after gaining full custody of Jason. He is raising his sons in Los Angeles.

Guess what? I love desserts and candy. Anything sweet makes me a happy man, but I still have a six-pack.

My guilty pleasure movie is Forrest Gump. I've seen it like 140 times. I love anything with young or old Tom Hanks. He's my celebrity crush.

You can't be an African American born to immigrant Jamaican parents and growing up in the South and identifying as gay at the age of eight without getting some tough questions. I knew that if I didn't want to be isolated and feel alone, I had to be open to people asking me questions that could be perceived as ignorant.

Kids would ask, "Why does your father's hair look like that?" of his dreadlocks. "Why is your skin so dark?" It's hard because you want to fit in and be just like everyone else. But what I realized was that if I wanted to have connections with people, I had to be willing to have conversations with them—and to say, "This is who I am. Let me learn about you." We're all going to have different views, but we can come together. Talk to me. I want to talk to you. I've been training myself to have hard conversations since the moment that I started talking. That's why I let people into my life regarding my sexuality at the age of fifteen.

THE MILLION-DOLLAR QUESTION

One day, about five years ago, I came home from my job as a licensed social worker and my younger son, Christian, who was thirteen at the time, was writing a paper on following your dreams. He looked up and asked me point-blank, "Dad, are you living your dreams?" I knew instantly that I was entering a pivotal parental moment. I could lie and say yes—my

My biggest pet peeve is people who don't show up, emotionally or physically. If you say you'll be there at two o'clock, be there at two o'clock. If I'm hurt, come to the house and see me. Don't just send me a text.

Who am I in three words? Open. Hardworking. Loving.

Number one on my life to-do list is to learn sign language.

Where will I be in ten years? Hopefully, I'm hosting Karamo Live!, my own daytime talk show. Many years after my talk show, I also see myself running for a political office—maybe governor of California—and right now, I'm learning about and getting involved in local and state issues.

nine-to-five job was fulfilling on a level, but it wasn't my dream. Or I could be honest and say no. So, in essence, I could either set my son on a path that I wanted him to be on, or I could set him on a potentially unfulfilling one that would be similar to mine.

So what *was* my dream? Ever since I was a kid growing up with three older sisters in Texas, I have wanted to be a talk show host. I used to record the Phil Donahue and Sally Jessy Raphael shows—and tape over my mom's soap operas, which got me in trouble many times—so I could watch them after school. I literally ran home as fast as I could to watch afternoon talk shows. I didn't even understand what they were talking about.

So what did I say to my son in that moment? It was as if someone had grabbed my throat. I told him the truth. Of course, his next question was "Well, why aren't you?" And so I asked myself that very same question. I didn't get more than two hours of sleep that whole night because my mind was going around and around asking, "Why not?"

The very next morning, I signed up for broadcast journalism night classes at my local community college. When I told my kids that dinner would have to be a little earlier and that I wouldn't be able to pick them up at basketball, they just shrugged. In my mind, going after my dreams had meant my life would shift and my kids would be devastated. Nah. I was wrong. But we all use excuses to avoid our truth.

FINDING YOUR CROOKED PATH

My granny used to say to me, "The day you stop learning should be the day you die." It sounds morbid, but basically what she was saying is that if you ever feel like you know it all, there's a problem. So going back to school for me meant I was going to do it, and I was going to do it right. I have to learn.

When I walked into the classroom that first night, the other students were so young—my kids' ages. I had this moment of asking myself why I would jeopardize my career, my life, and the savings for my kids' college funds for my dream. Plus, it was such a long shot—one in a million—that

I would land on TV. I didn't want to compete with these kids! I was exhausted. We all look at education as a young person's game. I was about to withdraw and walk out. But the teacher came in, looked at me, and said, "Ah, someone with experience." I still get chills when I think about those words because it reminds me that life gives you little signs, and if you are open to them, they might push you in the right direction. I literally pivoted and sat in the front of the classroom. I thought, "If I'm going to compete with these kids, I'm going to be right here because my eyesight's not so good." And in that moment, I knew that I was right where I was supposed to be. This was my path.

SOMETIMES "NO" MEANS "MAYBE"

As I mentioned, I fell in love with talk shows at a young age. When I got to college, I watched Oprah and saw that she was dealing with real issues about life, about family, about exploring the world around you. That was beautiful to me. I'm that person who likes to ask, "What are you thinking?" and "How can we fix a problem?" That's why I studied psychotherapy and became a social worker.

So in my mind, getting on TV meant a way to offer solutions. I wanted to give people advice they could use. That was always my end goal. I didn't want to be a newscaster. I didn't want to interview celebrities on the red carpet. I wanted to be with people and help them.

In my early twenties, I had been the first openly gay, African-American man on MTV's *Real World: Philadelphia*. I loved every minute of it, but I didn't learn any skills—the show didn't give me any formal training on how to be on television, and it didn't really give me the outlet I was looking for to help people. Besides, the nature of the show meant I was only on it for one season.

At class one night, I heard students talking about an audition for a new show at the Oprah Winfrey Network. I saw on the casting sheet that they were looking for a white male and two women of color. Still, I remember thinking, "This is my job. I know it. This is my job."

Now, that might sound arrogant. But I do think you need some ego to go after your dream. Not so narcissistic that you think you're better than everyone, but confident enough that you think you're deserving of an opportunity. At some point you have to believe that a dream job is yours—otherwise, you won't even go after it. Even though they were looking for a white guy, I said to myself, "I'm going to show up. This is my job."

So I went, and of course, the casting director said no to putting me on tape. But I went back the next day to the auditions and the day after that. You can't be afraid of a no. That was a big lesson for me to learn, especially in this business, but also in life. On the third day, she saw that I wasn't going to give up. I wasn't aggressive or rude; I was persistent, but charming and good-natured. She

Young Karamo in Texas

finally let me audition, and three days later, I got the job to be a host of *The OWN Show*. I'd reached a new threshold of my dream, but I kept my full-time job as a social worker for security and I kept going to class. Because like Granny said, you always have to keep learning.

CAN I LAND MY DREAM JOB?

So now I had education and experience, but I wanted to do a show where I could make a difference. By now, I had agents who would present me with auditions, and I would

say, "There's no solution there," and respectfully decline. There might have been a time in the past when I would've done anything to be on TV, but it was very clear to me that I had to stand firm in my conviction and not just go for the money. In my heart, I knew there was going to be something out there for me.

One night, I was watching TV and I heard *Queer Eye* was coming back. Again, I said to myself, "This is my job." I remembered that the original show had been critical in shaping our culture in the aughts and that those five gay men were going into people's homes and giving them solutions to feel better about themselves—and to help them relate to the world in a better way. It was exactly what I had been wanting to do for all these years.

I told the producers that I love theater and museums. But when I think about art, it's more art therapy than paintings and sculptures. I draw to relax. As a social worker, I used art therapy as a tool for people to have harder conversations with themselves. If I was going to

"I didn't want to be a newscaster. I didn't want to interview celebrities on the red carpet. I wanted to be with people and help them."

A glimpse of Karam's bomber jacket collection.

do *Queer Eye*, I knew culture had to be how I helped fix people on the inside. But that didn't mean sending people to museums and Broadway shows. I wanted to have deeper conversations with people so that they could have the hard conversations with themselves. The producers were hesitant because they didn't know how that process would translate on camera. But I was adamant that I had to give people on the show solutions to make their lives better.

When I told my kids I got cast on *Queer Eye*, their response was exactly what I expected it to be: "Great, can we go outside and play?" That has been their response to every job I've ever gotten. In that moment, I realized we all want people to have the same excitement we have about an accomplishment. But really, it's about how excited you are for yourself. Sometimes, at the end of the day, it's just you looking in the mirror and saying, "Good for you! You did it!" Let me tell you, I spent about twelve minutes brushing my teeth that night—just smiling at myself in the mirror.

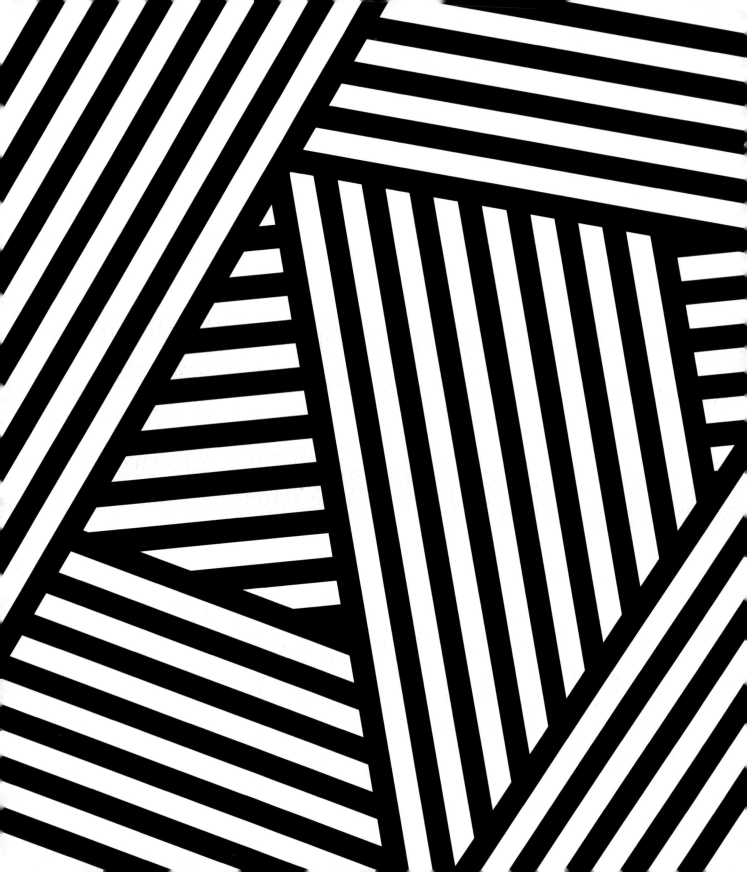

IT'S NOT A MAKEOVER; IT'S A MAKE-BETTER

Designing a better life is about far more than deciding what shirt to wear, which sofa to buy, or how to apply the right moisturizer. It's about creating a life that's well rounded, filled with laughs, lots of love, and a sense of personal achievement. Most important, it's about a life that best suits *you*.

One morning, you might need to selflessly show compassion to others, and on the next day, you just might need to take the perfect selfie that boosts your confidence. We live and breathe this philosophy of building a happy, healthy outer and inner life. Trust us, it's an ongoing evolution for everyone.

But the bottom line is about truly celebrating your best self every day. And in these next chapters, we're here to help you at every step along the way.

GORGEOUS, INSIDE AND OUT

Enhance your skin, hair, and soul

**R**epeat after me: Self-care is not vanity. Now say it again. I can't tell you how many times I speak those words of infinite wisdom to people every day. Why? Because so many of us—maybe even you—don't focus on our own well-being. We're too wrapped up in endless to-do lists and carpool duties and grocery shopping and board meetings and binge-watching *Walking Dead* for the eleventh time (okay, maybe that's just me—but you know what I mean).

We're all busy. So damn busy that we forget to take a moment to shine a light on our personal needs. That's my specialty. Unlike the rest of the Fab Five, I'm not measuring your waist for some cute skinny jeans or showing you how to flick the pit out of a luscious avocado. I'm the guy who says, "Settle down, honey. Close those gorgeous eyes. Take a moment to breathe." You would think my job would be the easiest. Poor Bobby is scrambling to carve a dining room table out of a freaking oak tree while all I'm asking someone to do is sit still. But you would be amazed at how hard it is for some people to relax and mindfully inhale and exhale. Try it right now. Go ahead. I'll wait.

Now, isn't that better? Don't you feel more connected to your body? So many people don't make themselves numero uno. Think about what they tell you on the airplane during that safety speech, you know, when the flight attendant says to put your oxygen mask on before helping anyone else. In other words, you can't do for others

until you do for yourself. That advice alone is worth your weight in those tiny packets of honey-roasted peanuts.

If you're wondering how self-care relates to beauty and grooming, relax. I'll get there. Remember, this chapter of the book is all about recharging, so we're not going to zip along like we're speeding to get to happy hour for half-price margaritas. Hmmm . . . though I would totally understand if you wanted to fix yourself one right now.

On the show and at the hair salon I co-own in Los Angeles, I see how an hour in a swivel chair can affect someone's mood, life perspective, and self-esteem. It's not just the new cut or the fresh buttery highlights either. Letting someone else take care of you—and perhaps gently massage shampoo into your precious baby scalp while you unwind—can be life-changing. I see heroes and clients alike literally transform from run-down and depressed to radiant and hopeful.

Now imagine if you could re-create that joyous feeling every day for yourself by indulging in a new skin-care regimen or a few moments of meditation while you wear a DIY hair mask. My goal here is to give you tips and show you the way to some me-time nirvana. Sure, I will also teach you how to get amazing, shiny hair that seems to bounce in slow motion and glowing skin that would make Karamo jealous. (Have you seen how light reflects off that man's cheekbones?) But ultimately, this journey is about going deep within because that's where we are all the most beautiful.

Ready? Now, let's start with some positivity.

BORN
BEAUTIFUL

The body image and beauty ideals we see on Instagram and TV and in magazines can make us feel downright deficient. They're all about how you look—and everyone wants to look perfect. We already talked about embracing imperfections. But still, I struggle with body image issues and then struggle with the fact that I'm still struggling with them. Enough already! You get caught up in negative self-talk and you start to spiral. Then, it's not just about practicing self-care. You need to give yourself a double dose of self-love.

For me, it helps to find little pockets of joy within the day to rest up and appreciate my body. Doing yoga, even for five minutes, reminds me of my strength. But if I'm really stuck and I can't do something physical, I just sit and breathe. When I inhale, I think about drawing in confidence or appreciation for everything I do have. When I exhale, I release fear or negativity or whatever it is that's consuming me. The important thing to remember is that you are special and you are beautiful. Remind yourself of that every morning and at night—and when you're stuck at a traffic light or waiting in line. You get the point.

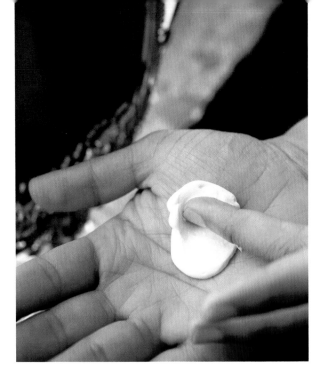

THE SKIN YOU'RE IN

Now let's make you glow. First things first: you have to get to know your skin intimately—"skintimately." As your biggest organ, your skin makes up about one-seventh of your body weight. It also works overtime to protect us from damaging UV rays and nasty free radicals and pollution ricocheting around in the environment. So before you can return the favor by showing your skin some TLC, let's determine its type so you can pick products that work best for you. A skin-care routine is the easiest way to practice daily self-care, but you can't achieve your skin goals if you don't know what your skin needs. Here are some clues to your type:

DRY: Your skin feels tight after you cleanse or when you wake up in the morning when it's dry. Your pores are almost invisible (lucky bitch!), and you may have more fine lines around your eyes and mouth.

Products and regimen:
Look for a cleansing oil, a hydrating serum, and a thick, creamy moisturizer, each of which will drench your dry skin with needed moisture.

OILY: Within twenty minutes of washing your face, you see shine on your forehead and around your nose and chin area; you may also see a residue on your phone screen. Your pores are usually enlarged.

Products and regimen:
Opt for a gentle cleanser that doesn't contain soap, exfoliate regularly, and choose a lightweight moisturizer like a gel lotion so you're not clogging your pores.

COMBINATION: You're like the Goldilocks of skin types—not too dry and not too oily. It usually means that your cheeks are dry but your T-zone area—the forehead, nose, and chin—gets shiny during the day.

Products and regimen:
Find a gentle balancing cleanser that won't strip your dry areas. Use a hydrating serum all over, but be sure to treat your T-zone with a mattifying product and moisturize with a gel or lotion formula.

SENSITIVE: Your skin turns red or flushes easily, and a new product can immediately cause inflammation. You may have a condition like acne, rosacea, eczema, or psoriasis. That's me, too. (More on me and my skin issues in a minute—right now we're all about you.)

Products and regimen:
Look for hypoallergenic products designed exclusively for sensitive skin and spot test any topical before you apply to your entire face. See a dermatologist if your skin is constantly irritated.

Here Comes the Sun Damage Show me your sunscreen, sweetie. I'm serious. Before I even look at your gorgeous skin and start playing with your hair, I want to know how you're protecting your face and your body from damaging rays. It is such a non-negotiable—even on cloudy days, when it's not all sunny out, you can burn. Freaky, I know. Get separate sunscreens for your face and body because you need to slather that protection for your body, from UVA rays (which cause premature aging and precancerous damage) and UVB rays (which cause sunburn), all over every square inch of skin. I literally buy that stuff by the gallon at Trader Joe's. For my face, I use a higher-end mineral sunscreen that's chemical-free—no parabens, no phthalates, no aluminum. The key is to put on sunscreen at least thirty minutes before you get in the sun. So don't think you can get all cute by the pool and then apply. Put it on before you leave the house or in the shade and call a friend and chat for a half hour while the SPF activates.

DO TOUCH YOUR FACE

Facial massage is a thing, and it deserves to be, well, a bigger thing. Stimulating muscles in your face doesn't just feel delicious; it also reduces tension and boosts your circulation, bringing more oxygen to the skin. Do it and you'll look more glow-y and toned. It's like a mini face-lift without all those bandages and recovery time—and it's cheaper! I'm literally massaging my cheekbones right now. Here's my method:

1 **Start from the bottom of your face,** above your jawline, and using the pads of your fingertips, massage upward in a circular motion to your cheekbones. You can add a little moisturizer or face oil to your fingers to make them glide easier, and vary the pressure by tapping your skin, too.

2 **Moving upward,** use your ring finger to make circles around your eyes and trace the orbital bone for five sweeps.

WE'RE ALL FLAWED

Perfection is boring. What's the fun in having no hairs out of place or an utterly symmetrical face with big soulful eyes, a gorgeous nose, and killer cheekbones? (Sorry, supermodels. Actually, not sorry.) We all have little imperfections—which I like to call "nuances"—that make us unique and sometimes even make us stand out. In my mind, that's a good thing.

Maybe it's a birthmark or a mole or a constellation of freckles across your nose. Or it could be a more obvious skin condition like eczema, acne, or model Winnie Harlow's condition, vitiligo, which is a disorder that causes skin to lose its pigment in places and appear much lighter than the rest of your complexion. I have psoriasis, which has been an issue for me since I had my first flare-up when I was twenty-three. I scratched an itch that became more and more inflamed—and it took *five* doctors to figure out what it was. Kim Kardashian and Cara Delevingne deal with it, too. Can you believe we all have so much in common?

Just recently, I kind of "came out" about my psoriasis. Not that I had been hiding it, but it wasn't something I highlighted on my social media. My condition is called guttate psoriasis, and I get dry, red patches and spots when it acts up. That day, on a photo shoot, I tried on a jacket that made my skin react. (Chemicals in new clothes can cause flare-ups.) I had a picture from the shoot to post, and at first I was going to edit out the spots. Then I thought, "My body is fierce and fine, and the more people that know about psoriasis, the more I can stop telling cute guys about it when I take my top off." So I posted the unretouched photo on Insta of me in a pair of boxer briefs and I called her out. So many people commented and reached out to me to say thank you or to ask me how I care for my psoriasis. Some sweeties asked me if it affected my self-esteem. FYI: I'm in a place of acceptance with it now; I'm just cool with it. But I wasn't always.

If you have a skin or hair condition that makes you self-conscious, you can get to that place of acceptance, too. When it bothers you, say some affirmations like "I'm enough," or meditate to clear your mind of negative thoughts. Remind yourself that you're as beautiful beneath the surface as you are in the mirror. There are positive role models who embrace their nuances. Look to them for inspiration.

Anyone who has browsed a cosmetics department or stepped foot in a Sephora knows there are like a gazillion cosmetic products out there. For some—like me—these stores feel like a candy shop. Others get overwhelmed with confusion. When it comes to makeup, I'm all about "less is more" and natural beauty. But there are a few basic products that can enhance your assets in seconds.

CREAM CON-CEALER AND COLOR CORRECTOR

Trust me. Once you conceal, the struggle is no longer real. Blemishes, dark under-eye circles, and sun damage vanish with one swipe. Just remember to moisturize your face before you dot on concealer, which can be drying. My philosophy on application is more area rug than carpeting, so blend it where you need it rather than automatically opting for full-face coverage.

BRONZER

All five of us wear bronzer on the show, but you can't tell, right? Who doesn't want to look like she spends her weekends in Hawaii? To apply, swirl a fluffy brush on the compact, shake off the excess, and lightly brush it where the sun naturally kisses your face: cheeks, chin, bridge of the nose, and forehead. Mwa.

MASCARA

Mmmm, honey! Extended lashes makes those eyes pop. If you have dark, full lashes, try clear mascara. For pale lashes, brown mascara applied to the top of your top lashes will elongate your eye. Here's a secret tip: Instead of pumping the wand to get more product, twirl it as you remove it from the tube. That way, less air gets in and the formula stays moist and lasts longer. You can also run the wand through a tissue to remove clumps and excess before you brush it on.

TINTED EYEBROW GEL

I call eyebrows a push-up bra for your face because a well-arched brow will literally make you look younger and better rested. Enough said? Enough said. Apply gel in short upward strokes in the direction of your hair growth.

NAIL POLISH

Antoni had his first pedicure a few months ago, and now he is ah-ddicted. He says that he loves a matte black on his toes, which is very badass, but he also goes for a frosty chenille pink from time to time. Who doesn't love to mix it up? A clear polish with a touch of pink makes your toes look naturally fresh and neat— and you can apply it yourself. For more adventurous men, I say visit a nail salon and experiment with bolder, masculine ones like navy and steel gray.

LIP MOISTURE

If you're going for color, I like a hint of gloss or tint that makes it look like you just bit your lip—in a sexy way. Karamo is never without his Carmex; my girl is ChapStick. Basically, flaky, dry lips are not kissable. Need I say more?

MAN UP WITH MASCARA

Guys, listen up. Before you get all heteronormative and tell me that makeup feels too fem, I want to educate you on the history of dudes and pretty pots and potions. As early as 4000 BCE, Egyptian men used pigment as black eyeliner—please notice that perfect cat-eye—and colored their cheeks and lips with red stain made from the mineral ocher. Roman men darkened their eyebrows with soot (crafty!) and used crushed poppy petals as blush in 100 AD. Cut to eighteenth-century France, where Louis XVI was known as the king who embraced his inner queen by powdering his skin and applying a fake beauty mark to his face. Oh, and Vikings were known to enhance their big blues with eyeliner. Call it your war paint!

FAKE A FLAWLESS SKIN TONE

Color correcting tweaks your little complexion imperfections. But don't be intimidated by a palette with purple, green, and peach shades. Remember the color wheel in grade school art class? Well, what each of these colors does is cancel out its opposite hue so you can achieve an even skin tone. Just be sure to dab product on lightly, whether you're spot correcting or altering overall skin tone, and blend like you mean it.

LAVENDER (PURPLE) cancels out yellow. Apply to brighten dull or sallow complexion.

GREEN cancels out red. Apply to subdue redness due to rosacea, broken capillaries, acne, or sunburn.

PEACH (ORANGE) cancels out blue. Apply to neutralize deep purple under-eye circles or blue veins.

Fake a Great Night's Sleep You skin doesn't keep secrets. If you hit the after-party hard last night, she's going to tell all. To make it look like you slept eight hours, start with an eye cream that contains tea tree oil or caffeine, which will stimulate circulation. You want to get that slow, tired blood moving and reduce the inflammation that causes swelling under the eyes. Softly apply the cream to your under-eye in outward sweeps, from the inside to the outside for about a minute. This is called lymphatic drainage and it breaks up the accumulation of fluid under your skin. Gross, right?

Next, take a jade roller (it looks like a mini paint roller and only costs about $8 online) and gently drag the crystal back and forth underneath the eyes to further de-puff, relieve any facial tension, and even improve elasticity. It may seem trendy right now, but FYI: This tool has been part of the Chinese beauty regimen since the seventh century. People say that it makes your moisturizer or serum penetrate deeper if you add product, but that's not true.

Finally, add a pair of eye gels or patches that contain hyaluronic acid, which is a substance that grabs moisture from the air. Peel them off after ten minutes, and your peepers will look completely refreshed.

Add a swipe of concealer under the eye to mask any dark circles.

HIP TIP *Spike your shampoo with a few dro[ps] rosemary or lemongrass es[sential] oil to stimulate follicles (... leads to hair growth) ar[d] treat a dry scalp.*

HIP TIP *Make any lipstick matte by dusting lips with loose translucent powder and then blotting with a tissue. Two pouts for the price of one.*

FEMINIZE YOUR FACE

Makeup artists and hairstylists can help transgender women in a transitioning journey that leads to a gorgeous emotional and physical transformation. We have magical powers when it comes to enhancing what any woman has already got. A few tips:

Avoid sheer coverage foundation, as the dewy finish will amplify any texture around the beard line. Instead, go with a full-coverage matte formula that you can gently press into the skin.

A touch of highlighter on the middle of the nose, forehead, and chin, along with a dusting on the tops of the cheekbones, will downplay any masculine facial features.

Wispy bangs artfully soften a high or wide forehead on any woman. Have your hair cut with layers around the face to blur a masculine jawline.

Transgender men, you can refer to the grooming tips throughout this chapter—they apply to you, too!

EAU DE FAB FIVE

A signature scent is your shortcut to notoriety. Your friends will come to recognize its spicy or floral notes, and it will linger for a moment after you leave—make them miss you, I always say. I asked my boys to share their secret scents. Notice how our scents match our personalities:

KARAMO: Dolce & Gabbana Light Blue. "It's the only cologne I ever wear, and it's been my scent for as long as I can remember. It's clean and fresh."

TAN: Vera Wang for Men. "I started wearing it at the age of seventeen. It's woody with cedar and classic and a scent that you would expect a lovely older gentleman to wear."

JONATHAN: "I'm obsessed with the sweet, bright citrusy notes of geranium oil, which I apply to my neck and wrists right after I shower."

BOBBY: Le Labo Santal 33. "I smell like leather and musk and it's very spice-forward."

ANTONI: Mojave Ghost by Byredo. "It's woody and musky with these sensual notes of violet."

The best way to find your signature scent is to go out and play with colognes, perfumes, and oils at a department store or apothecary. Make it a fun outing with a friend or a sexy activity with your partner. Just remember to use paper tester strips instead of your wrist because scents can easily overlap and muddle together. Once you find one that you love, apply it to your wrist and walk around for twenty minutes to get a true sense of its top and bottom notes (or essences).

YOU KNOW WHAT? I DON'T THINK ANYTHING IS REALLY EVER CUT AND DRY. IT'S ALWAYS A PROCESS. EVERYTHING IN LIFE IS A PROCESS. LISTEN TO YOURSELF BREATHE. IT'S A VERY GROUNDING, CALMING EXPERIENCE.

—JONATHAN

HIP TIP *To get an instant glow, do like Karamo and rub an ice cube tucked inside of a washcloth on your entire face until it melts. I would laugh, but have you seen Karamo's skin?*

SUNDAY FUNDAY

At the end of every week, I go into full "don't care, self care" mode. Sunday means a me-day marathon. First, I cleanse and exfoliate in the shower. I follow that up with an enzyme-resurfacing mask to tighten my pores and brighten up my complexion. Then, I move on to a moisture mask. Finally, I'll massage moisturizer into my skin and apply eye patches while I catch up on TV. Want to come over?

Here's my manuka honey mask recipe that can be changed up to suit your skin needs. FYI: Thanks to enzymes from bees, honey contains hydrogen peroxide, which is a natural antiseptic. Manuka honey also has antifungal properties because it comes from tea trees. These properties fight all the gross stuff (bacteria and pollutants) that collect on our skin every day. Gross, right? Yes, it has to be manuka—it's naturally more antibacterial and antimicrobial than normal honey.

EXFOLIATE Take a half cup of oats and pulverize them in the food processor. Next, add the oats to a cup of manuka honey in a bowl and mix well. Apply the mask in gentle, circular motion. **Leave it on for ten to fifteen minutes and rinse off skin with warm water.** *(Repeat this step for all of the masks below.)*

MOISTURIZE Substitute a mashed-up banana for the oats; the potassium will moisturize your skin and the protein lectin will destroy bacteria that can cause pimples.

ENRICH Substitute a mashed-up avocado for the oats to hydrate skin; the fruit's oleic acid reduces inflammation and softens lines. Yas, honey!

BRIGHTEN Replace the oats with two tablespoons of lemon juice or orange juice as a natural astringent to tighten pores, and the vitamin C will help to fade pigmentation and even out skin tone.

IT SHOULDN'T TAKE A VILLAGE

No matter what the tabloids like to say, stars are not just like us. They might brush their own teeth and turn the lights on when they get home, but when it comes to their hair, they have h-e-l-p. Professional help. That's not to say that you shouldn't dream big with your hair goals. I'm all for that triple axel approach to beauty and grooming. But when a client of mine with curly, chestnut-brown hair comes into my salon and asks for a pin-straight platinum-blond lob, I take a deep breath, sit her down, and ask, "Why, baby girl?"

It's part of the human condition to want what we don't have. I get that. When I was a little boy and longing for long hair every minute of every day, I also wanted it to be ruler straight. It's naturally curly and puffy. Flattening down frizz is not a huge ordeal, but when you're trying to

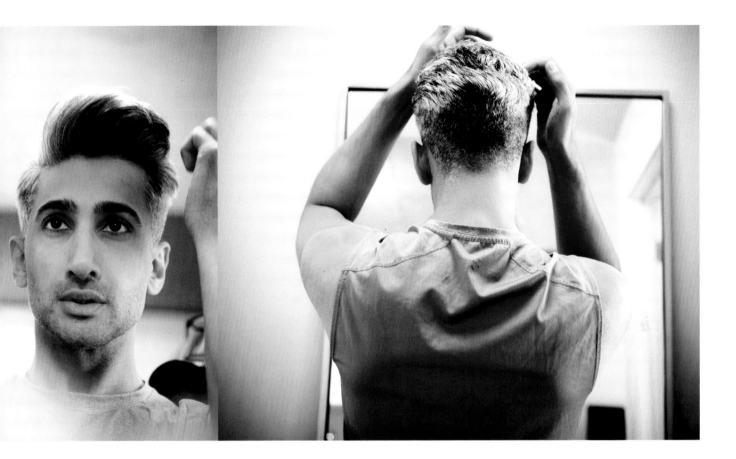

completely overhaul the natural color and texture of your hair, maybe it's time to practice a little self-acceptance. Celebrate what you have. Ask your stylist to help you find a way to work with your natural beauty. If your hair is wavy, try a style that works for that texture instead of flat ironing it every morning. That's a lot of heat!

Look at Tan. That dreamy silver hair of his is all natural—and it complements his mocha-nonfat-double-latte complexion perfectly. He gets that height with a dab of pomade and blow-dries his coif skyward with a round brush. ("It only takes me about five minutes, too," he says with a smile. Of course it does, Tan-Tan.) So if your hair is raven black, don't try to go ash blond. A severe change like that affects your overall coloring, including your skin tone. I believe that Mother Nature doesn't usually get it

too wrong, so don't battle what she gave you. Instead, just go with the flow.

And other times, we have to learn to work with what we don't have. When we first met, Karamo was coloring in his hairline because it was receding. He said he was ashamed. But his fix looked, um, unnatural. So the other boys and I staged a mini intervention to suggest that he let go and embrace his baldness—and he did. He's glad he did it, and now he knows that bald is sexy! He says, "I wish that everyone could have four honest brothers who tell them what's up." Aw.

Your hairstylist should always have your back. Before you discuss a style, he or she should ask you how much time you plan to spend on your hair in the morning. As a stylist, I don't want to create for you an elaborate look that calls for twenty minutes in the mirror if you'll have just four minutes to spare. Be clear and honest with your stylist about the time and effort you can commit to your hair. You have to account for maintenance, too. Highlights and color need to be refreshed. Certain cuts, like pixies and bobs, need more attention than long layers. Trust me, nobody loves a dramatic "before" and "after" more than I do. But even on the show, I'm careful not to do a transformation that's unrealistic for someone to attain without a village (or me) at his side. Your cut, your color, and your hair maintenance should all make sense for *you*.

Here are a few of my favorite expressions that I turned into hairstyles. Which one works for you?

THE STRUGGS TO FUNC:
This is a low- to no-maintenance look because you are literally struggling to function and can barely make it out the door in the morning. Avoid blunt lines that call for constant trims and flat ironing or over-the-top dye jobs that require crazy upkeep. Think simple and no fuss.

THE HENNY:
This is a cute—but not "trying-too-hard cute"—style that might involve some spikes up top or soft highlights and layers around the face. You don't need a ton of product or an arsenal of tools to make it happen in the morning, and the upkeep is low-maintenance.

THE CAN YOU BELIEVE?
The grand finale of hairstyles. It's big, it's bold, and it's anything but effortless. You are willing to spend hours in the salon and invest hundreds of dollars into making this look shine all the time. You don't even have to be anywhere in the morning. Think Beyoncé. Think Gaga—on her wedding day!

HIP TIP *Instead of spraying dry shampoo all over your hair, cover only the roots. First, spray along your part and then lift up individual sections of hair and continue to hit your roots.*

WHEN DIY MEETS TLC

I dare you to do a hair mask and a face mask at the same time. Refer back to my manuka honey face mask on page 101 if you're game to do double duty. But if you just want to tickle your tresses, these masks will strengthen your strands and make them super shiny.

The Hairtini Pour about a cup of agave nectar into a heatproof glass and place it in a pot of near-boiling water. You want it to get real runny. Next, mist your hair with aloe water or rose water to dampen and soften strands. Apply the nectar root to ends and comb through. After fifteen minutes rinse in the shower with water and then shampoo.

The Whip It Good Get a can of full-fat whipped cream. Don't even think about going for low-fat or non-fat—we're bingeing tonight! Spray whipped cream into your palm and work it through roots to the ends. Rinse in the shower after 15 minutes with water and then shampoo.

The Breakup People always ask me if you need to "talk" to your hairstylist before you move on to see someone new. The answer is no way, seize the day. We understand that sometimes you want to dip your toe in another hot tub, girl. It's natural. But if you plan to see a new stylist at the same salon—which can happen in a small town—you should let your person know beforehand and say "Thank you for everything" because that could be awkward AF.

LET'S BUST UP SOME RULES

I hate when people tell you what you can and can't do—especially when it comes to beauty and grooming. Women aren't allowed to have long hair after they turn forty? Tell that to Dolly Parton. Men with cute, spiky hair don't get taken seriously? Tell that to Bobby.

WASH YOUR HAIR EVERY DAY. K, no. Actually, daily cleansing with a detergent strips oils, which makes the oil glands in your scalp overproduce oil to compensate for the loss. I recommend washing twice a week and switching to a cleansing conditioner instead of a shampoo.

SPLIT ENDS ARE FRIZZ. Not at all. Split ends are caused by dryness that damages your hair shaft, while frizz is all about texture. I apply moisture cream to my ends before I blow dry to protect them from the heat. Also, if you have long hair, sleep with it up and away from your body, which also generates heat and causes dryness.

GET A TRIM EVERY SIX WEEKS. Unless you have a precise cut like a bob with bangs or a fade, you can see your stylist every two to three months. But go by and visit if you need some salon therapy.

Five-Minute Make-Better: Treat Your Feet

If your heels are dry and look like day-old buttermilk biscuits, try an exfoliant that contains an alpha hydroxy acid from a fruit component like pineapple extract or citrus. Apply your scrub after a bath or shower, because the moisture softens the skin, and then let it sit on your feet for a few minutes—take a minute to belt out a Solange song!—before you start working it in.

Scrub those heels and the bottoms of the feet with a washcloth or loofah. (The natural acid will start eating the dead skin cells.) After you rinse away the scrub, apply moisturizer and grab some fierce strappy sandals. For even more glow, apply moisturizer to your feet before bedtime and wear a pair of socks while you sleep.

Are We There, Yeti? Just so you know, I like body hair. But when it comes to your beard, there are some simple instructions that should sprout alongside that growth. First of all, wash it regularly, honey—and scrub it like you do when you shampoo your hair. Secondly, make it shine with beard oil, which conditions and softens hairs. (Experiment with cute scented ones that are infused with fragrances like vanilla, sandalwood, and citrus.) If you intend to style it or add texture, invest in a beard balm.

- If you're going to shave, you have to prep first. It's never just putting a razor to your skin. What you want to do is soften the cuticles of your whiskers so the blade will slide smoothly. Warm water and a lather of shaving soap will do the trick.

- Lastly, comb that beard like you would the hair on your head and trim it every week to maintain its shape.

- Luckily, the Fab Five loves some scruff, so check out our Instas for inspiration.

HIP TIP *Before you go to bed, apply eye cream—which is formulated for more delicate skin—to your neck and décolletage, where the skin is thinner and loses elasticity as you age.*

MIRROR, MIRROR

Define your personal style and build a wardrobe that makes you swagger with confidence

I need to use the F word: *fashion.* It's a term that brings to mind unsmiling supermodels stalking down runways wearing pleats, polka dots, and stripes—all at once. Unfortunately, it also intimidates the hell out of some people, so much that they avoid clothing racks at all costs. I happen to love fashion, but I'm not here to educate you on the history of haberdashery or to convince you to subscribe to *Vogue* or *GQ.* What I *am* here to do is help you find a personal style that makes you feel confident every single time you walk out the door.

Too often, we all get caught up in the idea of being "on trend." One season, high-waisted denim and crop tops are all the rage for women, and the next season the must-have look is pegged jeans and boy-cut blazers. For men, it's just as frenetic. I just can't keep up. Plus, slavishly following what is "in fashion" or "of the moment" doesn't really work for most of us. It makes you buy clothes that aren't necessarily right for your body type, and prevents you from developing your own true style. So you're not actually learning to dress yourself or have fun with fashion. Yes, it's true: The F word can be lots of fun.

That's where I come in. As a fashion designer and stylist, my goal is to help you find a signature style and looks that are right for *you*—and only you. Say you adore maxi dresses and they work for your body and you feel fantastic every time you slip one on. That's wonderful! Who cares if miniskirts the size of cocktail napkins were all over the runways

Too often, we all get caught up in the idea of being "on trend."

for this season? I believe that wearing what you love and what makes you feel unstoppable is always in fashion.

Many people see cultivating personal style as a shallow pursuit. They scoff at a pair of colorful socks or a tilted fedora. But I couldn't disagree more. I have built my whole life around the notion that making an effort and getting dressed appropriately can truly affect your life. If I dash out the door wearing an outfit that doesn't flatter my body or my coloring, I definitely don't feel like my usual chirpy self. (Trust me, nobody likes a brooding Tan.) It affects my performance, too. When I don't look my best, I skulk around and speak in monosyllables. But when I'm wearing an impeccable outfit that truly reflects my personality, I'm more outgoing and ambitious.

Now, enough about me. It's time to get dressed.

LET'S DEFINE YOUR PERSONAL STYLE

When I first meet you, I'm not judging your clothes—I promise you that. Yes, I may inwardly question whether those tattered cargo shorts make the best first impression or wonder why you're hiding your gorgeous hips in an A-line skirt. Really, what I'm doing is mentally assessing your silhouette. Are you tall or short? Lanky or well built? It's not that I want to change your body type, but it is your body type that will help determine which shapes work best to flatter your figure.

Next, I ask a few basic questions, like "What do you do for work?" and "How do you spend your free time?" Obviously, a banker needs more tailored and conservative looks than a deejay. (Lucky you, if you're a deejay! I love to dance.) If you attend fancy events like charity galas on the weekend, your closet will call for more formal wear than someone who likes to BBQ at home with the family or lounge on the couch.

After that, I want to know whose look truly excites you. Who do you look to for style inspiration? A personal style icon becomes your guide when you get dressed and when you shop. Maybe your icon is David Beckham, and you pull up pictures of him in slim-cut suits on your phone as you check out styles in a men's store. I call that "instant inspo." If you love Reese Witherspoon's Southern belle preppy style, analyze her wardrobe online and add her off-duty style staples like flowered sheaths and espadrilles to your shopping list. Your style icon doesn't have to be famous, mind you. It could be your effortlessly glamorous best friend, a colleague with a penchant for vintage, or even an uncle who always looks snappy. I typically advise that you pick someone of your gender, with your coloring, if you're just learning about style. Having an icon who shares those characteristics makes it much easier to choose colors and cuts that suit you. More advanced fashion lovers can cross basic parameters. Just study how that person puts together an outfit. Does she favor slim-cut jeans with silk blouses? Is he a master at layering dress shirts with sweaters and blazers?

Lastly, we get into specific preferences like color, patterns, cut, and style—it's all up to you, of course. If you tell me you love chartreuse, I love chartreuse. (Unless it clashes with your complexion, in which case we find a similar but more complementary hue.) You might feel confident whenever you wear a jumpsuit that cinches at the waist or a halter top that accentuates your shoulders. In that case, it's likely that you're showcasing your best assets without even consciously trying. Maybe you love dressing up, but hate the stuffiness of a tuxedo. These are all style clues that tell me how to enhance your wardrobe.

I liken this process to a big jigsaw puzzle. Now it's your turn to ask yourself those questions, or pose them to a friend or partner who may be struggling with his or her look. You can even fake my lovely accent to make it sound more official.

FOR THOSE WHO CLAP BACK

Every once in a while, someone scoffs when I ask about preferences and insists that he or she doesn't care at all about style. Usually, it's a man. I call bull on that excuse. Lurking beneath that disdain for clothing is either a lack of confidence or the belief that any interest in style makes a dude seem like less than a dude. Making an effort to look good does not make you effeminate. It's just you stepping up for yourself and for your partner. It's a sign of respect. That's something I wish I could personally tell every man on this planet.

HIP TIP *Don't buy anything without trying it on first. Also, always take three sizes into the dressing room with you (your size, plus one size up and one size down) since fits vary.*

MAKE-BETTER YOUR BETTER HALF

*When I first met my husband Rob, his go-to look con-*sisted of a quirky thrift store shirt with baggy jeans and slippers. Yes, fuzzy slippers. As Jonathan would say, "Can you believe?" Not only did I *not* believe, but also I actually bought him a whole new wardrobe within weeks. Bobby had a similar experience when he first met his husband Dewey in New York. Bobby says: "Oh my God! Dewey wore oversized flannel shirts and cargo pants. It was terrible. So I got rid of everything, and anytime I bought something for myself, I picked up the same piece for him in a different color. I wanted him to learn. Now I'm proud to say that Dewey actually has very good style. He's landed on his own."

If you have a style-challenged friend, colleague, or lover and want to help that person with an update, here are a few tips to get started:

LET THE FASHION VICTIM TALK FIRST. Ask her how her wardrobe makes her feel overall. Most likely, she will admit that she's not making an effort and it shows.

BE AS GENTLE AS A TROPICAL BREEZE. Point out the good, like a flattering color or a cool moto jacket that always looks sharp, before you launch into which pieces don't work.

INTRODUCE THE BASICS. Style is a lot like the alphabet—once you get the ABCs down, you can make big words. (See the capsule collections for men and women on page 121 for suggestions.)

TEACH, DON'T IMPEACH. The idea here is to empower this person to make his own personal style decisions, like Bobby did with Dewey.

GIVE A WINK. A genuine, pointed compliment—"Well done on the Windsor knot tie, mate!"—goes a long way.

"When I don't look my best, I skulk around and speak in monosyllables."

THE ESSENTIALS THAT GO EVERYWHERE

You know how you have certain friends who always make you feel taller and smarter? Or a roster of restaurants that never disappoint? Similarly, these classic-but-modern style staples work overtime for everyone and take the guesswork out of getting dressed. Here are my capsule collections that go beyond the call of duty.

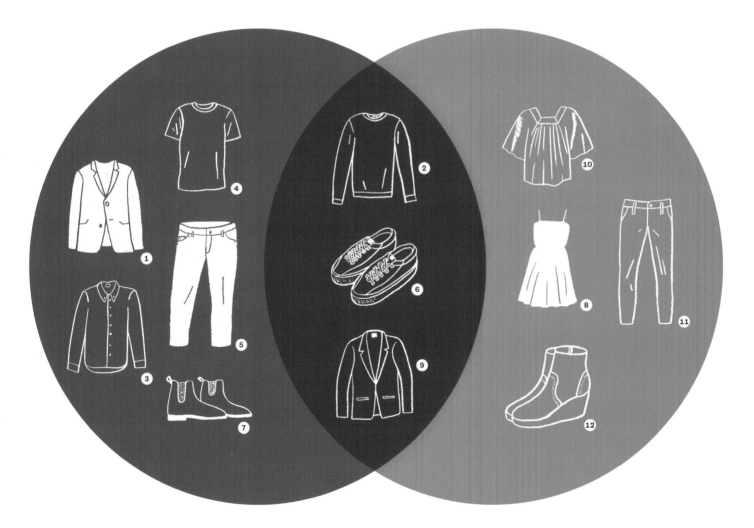

MEN

❶ DARK SUIT

It doesn't have to be black, and I personally prefer one with a faint pattern like a plaid or pinstripe, but be sure it's impeccably fitted to your body. *(A tailor is like a magician when it comes to making small tweaks that make a huge difference in the fit of your clothes. Find one in your area and you'll be surprised at how little it costs to have your clothes customized.)* You can swap out the blazer and pants as separates.

❷ CASHMERE SWEATER

You just can't go wrong with this impossibly soft wool fiber that comes from longhaired goats. This piece is an investment, but you can make it more formal with a collared shirt underneath or don it casually with a pair of jeans. Go for the most versatile crewneck style.

❸ CRISP WHITE BUTTON-DOWN WITH A COLLAR

It's fine to purchase a lower-priced shirt as long as it fits you well. Be sure to check out my instructions for how to master the French tuck, on page 129, in lieu of wearing a belt.

❹ CLASSIC FITTED CREWNECK

Grab a few of these jersey tees in neutral tones like white, gray, navy, and black. They make a traditional suit look ten years younger.

❺ DARK RINSE JEANS

Look for a modern, slim-cut style with stretch that slightly tapers at the leg even if you have never considered a more tailored fit. No slouchy dad denim or boot cut jeans, please. They broaden your silhouette and can make you look sloppy and dated.

❻ SNEAKERS

For men, I prefer a classic-style, white sneaker because it goes with everything. Just make sure you keep them pristinely clean. (Invest in white shoe polish . . . or even Mr. Clean Magic Eraser!)

❼ BOOT

A slip-on Chelsea style in suede pairs with everything and infuses a little rock in your roll.

WOMEN

❽ LITTLE BLACK DRESS

You might be rolling your eyes because this staple tops every magazine must-have list. But there's a reason for that: If you buy the right LBD, you can wear it everywhere. I love one in a patterned fabric like jacquard to make the simple frock stand out, or a structured ponte double-knit fabric that flatters curves. Just be sure to get creative with accents so it doesn't become "little black drab." I love an LBD with a white leather moto jacket or gold booties.

❾ BLAZER

No piece is more transformative than a well-cut, light jacket that dresses up denim and puts a professional spin on a party dress. Look for one with a hem that skims your hipbones, which is most flattering and versatile.

❷ CASHMERE SWEATER

This piece will require more of a financial outlay, but cashmere wears well and feels like a self-care reward against your skin. I recommend a V-neck for women, as the style looks a bit more formal with a pair of jeans.

❿ BLOUSE

Your version of this staple could be the classic white button-down, which will get lots of mileage underneath a cashmere sweater, or perhaps you prefer a more statement-making maroon silk top with a bow at the neck. Consider which is more appropriate for your workplace and try your top on with your denim and sweater.

⓫ TAILORED DENIM

Flared, wide-legged, slim-cut—the style is entirely up to you as long as the fit looks made-to-measure. Jeans with a dark rinse—no fringe, no whiskering, don't even ask about acid wash—look the most polished and can double as trousers.

❻ SNEAKERS

You beautiful women seem to do the most running around, so treat yourself to a chic pair of stylish and comfortable kicks. Opt for leather (which is easier to keep clean) so you can pair them with tailored pants and dresses. I prefer kicks in black or white so they don't become the focal point of your outfit.

⓬ BOOTIES

Consider this style a modern-day pump. An ankle boot with a wedge or high heel effortlessly transitions from your tidy desk to an unruly dance floor.

These recommendations are hardly random, mind you. Each separate should be considered a building block in creating a look for day or night. As a devout baker (see my recipe for divine carrot cake on page 222) I liken these pieces to flour, sugar, eggs, and butter. They're versatile and can be mixed and matched and dressed up or dressed down. Now let me show you how to have fun with your new wardrobe.

HIP TIP *If you're shopping and in between sizes with a beloved brand of jeans, round down. Denim always stretches.*

MIX AND MATCH

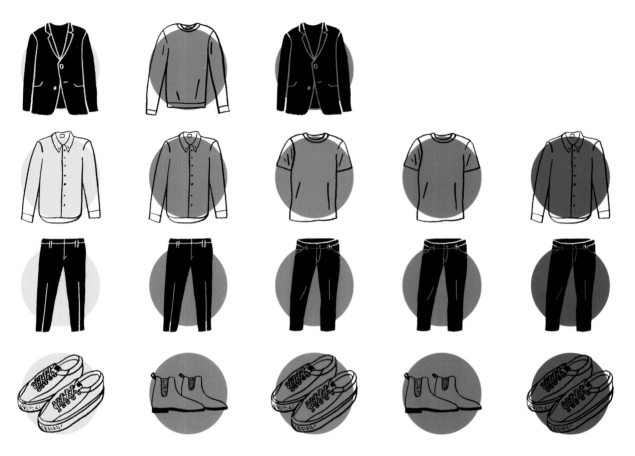

Men, let's start with that basic dark suit. Beyond the more formal look when the jacket and pants are worn together with the button-down shirt, you have a pair of tailored trousers that work with that same crisp white shirt and your cashmere sweater. (Vary that ensemble even more by substituting a crewneck tee for the button-down underneath the sweater.) Dress it up with the boots or add casual flair with your sneakers. Already, we're up to six different outfits, mate!

Your suit jacket doubles as a blazer and can be paired with your jeans and the button-down (with or without the sweater) or the crewneck tee. Again, take it up a notch

with the boots or make it more "street" by adding sneakers instead. Now we're up to a dozen looks.

Take away the suit jacket and wear the jeans with any of the three combinations listed above and you have another three possibilities. With just these seven pieces, you're able to create enough daily looks to last nearly two weeks. Also, any new clothes you buy—from a print button-down to a pair of corduroys—can be plugged into the same combinations.

On to the ladies. You, too, can mix and match with your separates. Pair the LBD with the blazer and booties for a polished professional look, and simply ditch the blazer

to make it more nighttime-appropriate. By the way, certain sneakers, like slip-ons, look cool with mini-, midi-, and maxi-dresses. If your cashmere sweater works atop a dress, you have another look. Otherwise, drape it over your shoulders and tie the sleeves in front to give it a collegiate twist. That's five looks and we have so many more combos to try.

Your dark, fitted jeans and blouse take you to a business lunch when you add your booties. Or pair the denim with just the cashmere sweater. Add the blazer for an evening event or layer the cashmere sweater on top of the blouse. Make any of the above ensembles a sporty weekend brunch look by subbing in your sneakers for the booties. You're up to thirteen lovely looks. Love it!

But again, this is just the beginning. These basics easily adapt to new additions. For instance, a cool, fitted T-shirt can be worn casually with the denim and sneakers or amped up with the blazer and booties. Pick up a pair of tailored black pants and sub them in for all of the denim equations. Once you acquire the essentials and get comfortable playing with different style medleys, you can branch out to more sophisticated separates like pencil skirts and cropped denim jackets. Look at you go, lovely.

MAKING AN EFFORT IN ONE AREA OF YOUR LIFE, LIKE DRESSING IN CLOTHES THAT LOOK GOOD AND FIT WELL, CAN AFFECT SO MANY OTHER AREAS OF YOUR LIFE. IT'S AN AMAZING RIPPLE EFFECT. JUST TRY IT.

—TAN

HIP TIP *Shop out of season to save as much as 75 percent on classic investment pieces that never go out of style, like designer coats, boots, and cashmere sweaters.*

DENIM FIT GUIDE FOR MEN

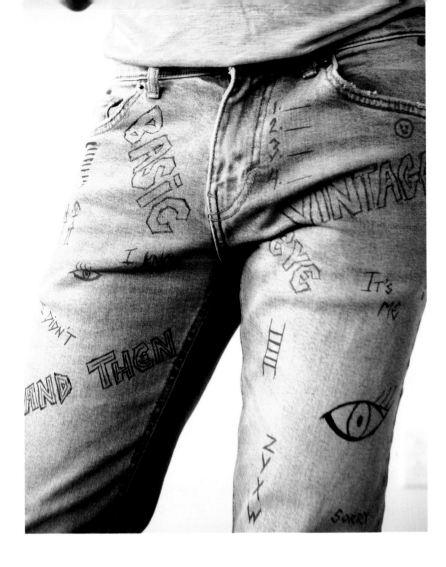

As you already know, I'm a fierce fan of slim-cut jeans for men. I can't even tell you what a tapered style does for a man's physique. Before you protest that you're out of shape or too stout to go slim, know that many denim companies now offer different versions of more narrow styles for everyone. Be sure to try on each option to see which fit feels right for you.

SLIM: Most narrow fit from hip to ankle, with a narrow thigh fit and skinny fit in the leg.

TAILORED: Regular fit in the thigh with a tapered leg.

ATHLETIC: Extra room in the thigh and the seat, with a slightly tapered leg.

DENIM FIT GUIDE FOR WOMEN

CUTS

Every season, on-trend denim styles change for women. But don't bother with fads. Instead, experiment with these five basic cuts that never go out of style, and find the rise that feels most comfortable.

SKINNY: This style hugs the hips, thighs, and legs all the way down to the ankle and is especially elongating with a pump or high-heel bootie.

STRAIGHT: Unlike skinny, this cut has more room in the knee and ankle and pairs well with polished kicks or loafers.

KICK FLARE: Typically high-waisted, these jeans feature a slight flare that should hit two inches above the ankle. Wear them with platform heels or high-heeled sandals to add edge.

WIDE LEG: Roomy but still tailored, this cut looks great with a tucked-in button-down shirt and chunky shoes to balance the proportion of the pants.

BOYFRIEND: Baggy by design, these jeans have ample room in the waist and thigh and should be rolled at the hem to fall about three inches from the ankle. Add feminine shoes like ballet flats or sandals to contrast the masculine cut.

RISES

The rise is, in essence, the length between the crotch seam and the waistband. Exact measurements vary by design, so I always suggest you try on each style to see which rise feels right.

LOW-RISE: The waistband sits at least two inches below your belly button.

MID-RISE: The waistband sits less than an inch below your belly button.

HIGH-RISE: The waistband sits anywhere from an inch to two inches above your belly button.

There's an art to looking stylishly undone but still like you made an effort. The French tuck is my answer to achieving that style. All you need to do is tuck in your shirt *ever so slightly* only in the front and leave the back shirttails loose. This move lengthens your legs, reveals just enough of your waist, and makes any outfit look smarter.

The no-show-laces tuck has the same effect, but on your feet—it elevates the look of sneakers or any laced shoes or boots. Simply make sure your crisscross laces are taut and then tie a bow behind the tongue of your shoes or kicks. Then, tuck your laces underneath the tongue so it disguises any loose ends.

No one likes sloppy bunny ears. Tuck in your laces for a clean look.

BLURRED LINES

Women have always borrowed style cues from men. Think of Marlene Dietrich and Madonna in killer power suits, or Diane Keaton in *Annie Hall*, wearing a flounder-wide tie with a men's vest. Women understand that the juxtaposition of the masculine and the feminine is incredibly sexy. There's even a style of denim and sweaters for women called "the boyfriend" that fits loose and baggy. Jonathan always says he loves a cute, baggy boyfriend jean, even though he doesn't have a boyfriend . . . yet.

Isn't it time we men started dipping our toes into androgyny more often? Or embraced a more gender-neutral stance on fashion? I tried on my first crop top a few years ago and I've never looked back—it's one of my favorite looks now. Antoni wore a vintage kimono out and about that practically caused a collective fashion orgasm online. In the spirit of equal rights—which I loudly and proudly support—I'd like to encourage more so-called "drag." Both Jonathan and I wear women's jeans because they fit us better and the denim is usually softer. When I can't find the right cut in a sweatshirt, I'll saunter over to the ladies' section for a more fitted version. You may not be ready to follow me, but here are ways to stylishly get in touch with your feminine side.

SMELL THE ROSES A floral patterned button-down softens the severity of a dark suit or black jeans. If that's too flowery for you, start off with a floral tie or pocket square.

STAY GOLD I'm a huge fan of jewelry for men and wear multiple rings and bracelets. They add points of interest and a fiery flash of metallic—just don't take it to the Liberace level with every knuckle adorned. Antoni and I went to a jewelry making party for my birthday one year and created these chic enamel bracelets that add a shot of bright color to any neutral or monochromatic look.

SHOW SOME LEG In a skirt? Yes, a skirt! Jonathan loves a kilt ("He kilt it," we like to say!), which very manly Scottish men traditionally wear to formal events. But Jonathan wasn't 100 percent on wearing a skirt until he took a chance, right? He thought it might look too crazy, but then he put it on and felt amazing. FYI: Bus drivers in France recently skirted around a "no shorts" policy by wearing wrap skirts during a brutally hot summer. You should try it!

BAG IT I can't bear to see a man's lean, striking silhouette made bulky because of pockets filled with keys, a phone, loose change, and who knows what else. A small or medium cross-body bag—just please don't call it a man purse—is the ideal way to tote personal items and techno essentials.

THINK PINK Pastels like salmon or mint green pair well with neutrals and add a refreshing lightness to a summer look. Just don't overdo it in head-to-toe tangerine.

DON'T SWEAT IT

Once upon a time, you wore slacks to work and sweatpants to work out. Then along came "athleisure." This fashion marriage of gym clothes and casual wear has become a billion-dollar industry and as someone who hits the gym every morning, I'm all for it. And really, who doesn't love wearing clothes as comfy as pajamas? The key to looking sporty chic and appropriate outside of a spin class, however, is to add polished pieces. For instance, ladies can amp up a pair of track pants or Lycra leggings with a button-down and a blazer or a belted boxy jacket, or a classic moto jacket does the trick, too. Add ankle booties to make the whole look more sophisticated.

For men, it's more about fit and modern cuts. I don't care for baggy hoodies and sweatpants with enough room to shoplift a six-pack of beer. Tapered joggers and slim-cut track pants pair perfectly with a leather-trimmed or suede bomber jacket—thanks for the inspo, Karamo. A dark denim jacket layered over a button-down and a fitted tee elevates casual track slacks as well. Pullover sweatshirts and jersey zip-ups work in the office when you add a modern, unstructured sports jacket. Oh, and be sure to trade in those battered gym sneakers for a pair of slip-on boots or pristine white kicks.

WATCH WHERE YOU'RE GOING

Being from around London and a longtime fan of its urban street style, I'm obsessed with looks that don't originate on the runways and red carpets. Just stroll through any city and you'll spot people expressing their personal style in a way that usually celebrates their surroundings, traditions, and culture. When I travel, I even jot down notes if I see a great look, so I can bring it home with me. My favorite cities for checking out street style run the gamut, from Hong Kong to Chicago to London to Salt Lake City. My point is, you don't need to jet off to Paris to pick up some urban inspiration.

HIP TIP *Elevate a boring suit—skirt or pants—by swapping out a classic neutral button-down for a boldly printed dress shirt or even a bright polo.*

FASHION FOR YOUR FACE

Neither Jonathan nor I believe that your makeup must precisely coordinate with your clothes. Matchy-matchy is for toddlers. But there are a few color combinations that look spectacular together. Here are our favorite alliances:

NAVY WITH METALLIC A deep blue dress or pantsuit gets enhanced with a softer, smoky bronze, gold, or copper eye.

RED WITH RED A red frock, sweater, or suit with a bright red pout is a gutsy double sucker punch of sexy.

JEWEL TONES WITH NUDE A striking sapphire, amethyst, or emerald sheath shouldn't compete with a bold lip. Instead, go with a nude pucker.

BLACK WITH BURGUNDY The classic all-black ensemble with bright red lips gets a moody, vamped-up spin when you choose a dark oxblood lipstick instead.

"I have built my whole life around the notion that making an effort and getting dressed appropriately can truly affect your life."

Now that you have a grasp on style, it's time to pick a lane or a signature look that personifies your image. This is your chance to refine what you have learned and make it more reflective of you. Think of Anna Wintour with her razor-cut bob, bangs, and oversized sunglasses, or Pharrell Williams's artistic getups and big, bold hats. I consider this kind of thing to be a fun calling card that makes you more recognizable. When you add this element to your ensemble and take a look at yourself in the mirror, you should instantly think, "Wow. This is so *me*." That dedicated piece of clothing or flourish brings you closer to who you are—or want to be—and creates confidence. It says to the world that you know how you want to be perceived, whether it's sporty or sophisticated.

Having a signature look or accent also makes it much easier to shop with purpose. If your go-to happens to be bold accessories like bangles and chunky necklaces, the jewelry department becomes your first stop online or in a boutique. If you feel like your best self in colorful high-top sneakers, you can easily figure out where to get the latest designer kicks.

That signature often becomes your starting point when you get dressed, making it easier—think of it almost as a uniform. Look at Karamo with his bomber jackets. (Seriously, he owns about three hundred of them!) He has created a unique individualized look that captures his personality and his style. It's laid back, but polished and versatile. When he gets dressed, he picks out his bomber first and builds an outfit around it. If you're looking for a signature highlight that works professionally, consider a bomber or a cardigan or an unstructured blazer—presuming your workplace isn't too formal, of course. I love a piece of outerwear that amps up a day-to-day look.

Can your clothes tell your story? Absolutely. Take Antoni, who rocks his arsenal of T-shirts rather brilliantly. I can't wait to read what he's wearing across his chest, whether it's a band name or a quote from a book. But there's more to his outfits than meets the eye. What do we learn when we see his shirts? Well, he's very passionate about music, and his style allows him to showcase bands he loves, like the Strokes and the National. Antoni also never leaves home without his vintage 1955 Omega watch because it speaks to his love for craftsmanship and antiques. See? We know Antoni a lot better just by assessing his style.

Sometimes, a signature telegraphs a cultural leaning and can identify you as part of a tribe. When Karamo first came out, for instance, he realized that he was straddling two pivotal cultural roles—one as a gay man and another as an African-American male. His fitted caps were the first thing he started wearing that he felt connected him to the hip-hop

HIP TIP *Bypass a bow tie to make a tux look more modern—just remember to leave the top button of your shirt open. A turtleneck with a tux brings out the James Bond in any man.*

culture. He says, "When I wore that first cap, I remember the way that African-American men looked at me like I was one of them. It made me feel validated and it's always become my security blanket since then."

Of course, Jonathan—whom we refer to as "our baby boy"—loves to keep us guessing with his style. He can transition from his daily uniform of skinny jeans with a suede boot and long-sleeved tee to a vintage caftan with killer gold sequin heels. "Life's too short to be boring," he says, as if we didn't already know he lives by that motto.

But in wearing heels with a pair of jeans and a T-shirt, Jonathan broadcasts that there really are no rules when it comes to fashion and gender norms. I absolutely love that! His signature style makes that important statement.

What I appreciate about Bobby's low-key signature palette of gray, navy, and other dark colors is that it speaks to his dedication to his work—and his reluctance to overshadow the interiors that he creates. Obviously, you wouldn't wear a pristine white button-down or velvet blazer when you're refinishing cabinetry. Still, he

manages to saw boards in half while looking smart and stylish. His preference for classic, comfortable staples like fitted polos and sweatshirts signifies that he's someone active, with a job that calls for functional clothes. A perfect example of your signature style working for you, not the other way around.

Oh, you want to know about me? Well, if you insist. You may think I obsess over short-sleeve print shirts, and yes, I do love a graphic pattern. But my signature style is always evolving. Every couple of seasons, I change up my look just because it's fun to reinvent myself. That's precisely why I changed my clothes so many times in a day as a little boy. I'll never dress too stuffy. You won't catch me in a suit unless it's a strict dress code—and I'll always wear it with sneakers. I'll always be a fierce fan of the French tuck, too. But otherwise, expect the unexpected. Maybe my signature style is to keep you guessing what I will wear next.

Karamo's hat collection plays a fun supporting role to his colorful bomber jacket collection.

Five-Minute Make-Better: Get Vertical

Obviously, a pair of three-inch heels will literally make anyone taller—and extend your silhouette. But there are more nuanced ways to seemingly add a few inches vertically, which will make you look longer and leaner overall. Here are my go-to stylist tricks that take you to the final stretch:

MAKE IT MONOCHROMATIC Dress head to toe in one hue—preferably a classic neutral like gray or camel—so the eye doesn't stall at a change of color. (The same rule applies for a bold shade like red or sapphire blue.)

GO AU NATUREL For ladies, a nude shoe, particularly a pump that matches your skin tone, extends your leg line. Pointy shoes do, too. Men, be sure your shoes don't contrast too much with your pants because it shortens the leg. Think black denim with dark sneakers or boots.

HACK YOUR HEMLINE A skirt that falls just above the knee also makes your legs look longer. Similarly, a maxi-skirt that cinches at your natural waist and grazes the floor makes you look taller.

SUIT UP SMARTLY A shorter jacket exposes more leg and lengthens a man or woman's silhouette. Also, opt for a two-button jacket with buttons above the waist to have the same effect as above. Narrower lapels elongate the frame, too.

PLAY WITH OPTICS Paneled dresses or shirts with contrasting designs that skim your silhouette deceive the eye into seeing a longer figure.

GET A LEG UP A tapered or slim-cut pant leg is always more flattering than fabric that puddles at the top of your shoes. Avoid cuffs or rolled pant legs that shorten legs, as well.

GO TOP HEAVY Don't laugh, but a towering topknot actually adds three inches—thank you for the tip, Jonathan. Spiked hair or a pompadour or a high fade like my style raise you up, too.

HIP TIP *Men can make the eye dance away from a burly midsection by layering shirts and jackets, which draws the gaze upward.*

LET'S BE REAL

Achieve your best life with a game plan and realistic goals

**D**id you know that women cry an average of five times a month, while men cry only about once per month? From what I've heard, people who watch *Queer Eye* are crying plenty more than that. But we don't stir up these deep, deep feelings in you when you watch the show just to make your nose run. We do it because it's not enough to simply get "in touch" with our emotions. In my opinion, that's only the beginning, the first baby step. We want you to engage meaningfully with your feelings and explore what those emotions are trying to tell you. That's the real work, the marathon. That's what makes your mascara run.

As the show's culture expert, my goal is to help people become the most authentic versions of themselves. It's for sure a different direction from the first incarnation of *Queer Eye*, where the focus was on more of an introduction to the arts. Hey, I love *Hamilton* as much as you do, and I take my sons, Jason and Christian, to museum exhibits all the time. But the reality is that you can't fully appreciate the finer things in life if you're not living your best life. So this time around, the idea is to help fix the inside and make a real connection with everyone we meet. If we end up taking a dance lesson or hitting up a gallery, that's an added bonus.

Here's how it works: When the Fab Five sweep into a hero's life, I step back and let my four beautiful brothers size up the physiological

needs first. All the while, I am assessing the psychological situation. Maybe our hero needs a shirt that fits. Maybe it's time he or she learned how to make a healthy, delicious dinner. While that's being sorted out, I stand back and take mental notes on our hero's internal situation. Is he slouched in front of the bathroom mirror and avoiding his reflection? Does she look sad when she talks about her relationship with her mother? When I see those signs, I'm on it with solutions to help that person face a life dilemma.

But I don't hang up my bomber jacket and stop working when we finish taping *Queer Eye* at the end of the day. No way. Making connections with people has always been my mission—it's why I became a social worker after college. I'm constantly striving to have deeper and more culturally relevant conversations with people around me so they can have hard conversations with themselves. Trust me, every day I have those difficult discussions with myself, too. That's how you grow and become more confident in who you are—or who you want to be. Then, you can go out and have those hard conversations with the world. Think of the impact we can have on the future.

This may sound like heavy stuff to tackle, but I believe in you. Plus, I'm right here to help you start. I'll even answer some tough questions along the way. I promise you won't even need a tissue.

YOU CAN ACHIEVE ANYTHING

When I hear people say they feel stuck or uninspired in life, my first question is "What do you want?" So many times, they don't have an answer. They might know what they *don't* want—whether it's an unfulfilling relationship or a cluttered home—but they haven't outlined a goal, like being in a loving partnership or living in an organized space.

So let's do this right. Start by acknowledging what you want. Say it aloud so you hear your goal. Write it down and put it somewhere you will see it every day. And be specific. Something like "I want a better life" will overwhelm you. Instead, think about what, on a micro level, will make life better. What's something you can achieve? Will more friends enrich your life? Or would a better-paying job enhance your life by enabling you to travel?

Let's take Tan's story as an example. He resolved to start his own business at the age of twenty-three. He even had a vision back then of selling it by the time he turned thirty-five so he could raise a family, which is exactly what he plans to do. Maybe it's more of an internal pursuit, and you want to work through the pain of a breakup or some form of rejection. Make sure this achievement is truly important to you by also writing down the motivation behind it. Why is this goal a valuable pursuit in your life *right now*? Whatever it is, state it loud and proud.

Next, it's time to implement my "Plan, Do, Ask for Help" approach. (I need to make Antoni wear that on a T-shirt!) My sons joke that I say those words almost every day—and I probably do. But this philosophy got me to where I am today. Remember how I talked earlier about chasing down my dream to help people on TV? Without a game plan, action, and help from my community, I wouldn't be here with you now.

Making a plan sounds daunting. Instead, think of it more as making your goal actionable. Whatever you wrote down on that piece of paper, we need to make it measurable. If your goal is to make new friends or increase your income, assess realistically how many people you want to meet or how much more money you want to make. Quantifying what you need to do makes it more realizable. Now, let's be real: How are you going to do that? Maybe you join a local club to meet new people, or RSVP yes to that party you are kind of dreading. Or perhaps it's time to finesse your résumé and start sweeping recruiting websites online.

Once you make that "plan" related to your goal, you can start "doing" those things to get closer to your objective. It's okay to start small—that's why we made the plan in the first place. All those small steps will add up and get you to the finish line. You have a timeline that charts those steps so you stay the course.

If you feel lost along the way, "ask for help." Never forget that people around you, like me, are here to support you. Bobby relied on so many friends (some of whom he even met online) and colleagues to help him get out of his hometown, eventually move to New York, and then build his incredibly successful business. Help doesn't make you weaker; it makes you stronger.

The more you vocalize and envision your goal, the more real it will become in your mind.

ADULT EDUCATION

When it comes to schooling, we all learn how to read, write, and multiply. But what about life skills? I'm talking about the tools we need to navigate this world. None of my teachers in rural Texas touched on the tricky stuff like standing up for yourself in a negotiation or asking your neighbors for a hand. With that in mind, here are life lessons worth learning and living right now.

DON'T BE AFRAID OF NO. A lot of times, people are so fearful of that tiny, two-letter word that it stops them asking for anything at all. You *will* hear no in your life—and sometimes it's worthwhile to readjust and reframe your approach by asking in a different way. For every twenty denials, you'll get at least one yes. Just ask Bobby. In his home décor business, he hears from builders and contractors all the time that they can't meet his timeline or budget for a renovation. So he goes back with a new ask until he hears what he needs to. Stay the course and let *no* push you harder.

LEARN HOW TO BUDGET. I'm not just talking about your finances. It's more about budgeting your time. Do you prioritize time for yourself to make accomplishments? Better yet, do you even have the time to put a plan in action? As a single dad who shifted careers in his thirties, I had to figure out how to make time to go back to school. That meant shifting priorities, like seeing friends, until I finished my studies. After Jonathan lost his stepfather and gained seventy pounds in three months, he decided to put his health first and foremost by working out with a goal. He went on to get certified as a yoga teacher (which means he devoted three hundred hours to studying the discipline) to strengthen his practice and share something he loves.

EMBRACE YOUR COMMUNITY. Everyone has hopes and dreams. If you reach out to other people, you can learn from their experiences. Ask, "How did you do it?" and "What did you learn along the way?" You can also get the support you need. When I was going to school at night, my neighbors pitched in and picked up the kids from basketball for me. When Antoni heard about the reboot of *Queer Eye*, he turned to his mentor Ted Allen (who just happened to be the food and wine expert on the original show) to ask for pointers before he auditioned. It's not cheating; it's being resourceful.

NEVER STOP LEARNING. Whether it's pursuing formal education or just going online and reading, keep expanding your knowledge. Explore what you don't know. Jonathan hosts a weekly podcast called *Getting Curious* where he interviews everyone from a professor of Middle Eastern history to a specialist on the Chinese economy. He's actually something of a scholar. Just don't get sucked into what I call the deadly Facebook algorithm or learning bubble, which means that you are only feeding yourself information that serves your ego.

DON'T MAKE ASSUMPTIONS ABOUT OTHERS. People are more than just labels. Don't presume you know someone's story because she is a lesbian or because he has tattoos. We are all much more than our appearances and our professions and even our political parties. To connect with people, look behind your assumptions and interact in a shared human experience.

HIP TIP *"XO" is not a proper or professional email sign-off in the workplace. "Respectfully submitted" or the classic "Sincerely" or "Best" hits the right note.*

KIDS SHOULD BE SEEN *AND* HEARD

I came from one of those families where kids were better seen and not heard. It was like, "Hush. Grown folk are talking." I was never encouraged to speak. That always bothered me—and maybe it's why I love to talk my feelings through now. And it affected how I raise my sons, too. They know they can always share their opinions with each other, with me, and with other adults. They also know my guidelines for a meaningful dialogue.

That said, they are not allowed to be disrespectful. Interrupting someone, using profanity, or attacking an individual's idea or stance on an issue is forbidden. It doesn't matter how differently or passionately they might feel about a topic.

Also, my sons know they have to listen as much as they talk. It's natural to want to share your views, but you miss out on a lot when you don't take the time to hear other people. That doesn't mean nodding while you're thinking of what to say next. Eyes open. Ears open.

Discussions are not school debates. The prize here is to teach someone a new perspective or to learn a fresh viewpoint on an issue yourself. Ultimately, you win when people come together.

Finally, I always remind my sons that their thoughts are valid. Kids may be less experienced and even immature in their sensibilities, but they're still human beings. Chris and Justin know that they have every right to contribute to any conversation.

"I'm constantly striving to have deeper and more culturally relevant conversations with people around me so they can have hard conversations with themselves. Trust me, every day I have those difficult discussions with myself, too. That's how you grow and become more confident in who you are—or who you want to be."

—KARAMO

CAN YOU HEAR ME NOW?

Don't even get me started on cell phones. As someone who makes it a priority to engage meaningfully with others, the constant texting and scrolling and snapping selfies is a huge issue. People, your phone is not your friend or your wife or your child! And yet I see so many of you pay infinite attention to it. Guess what? I'm guilty, too. I find myself patting my pocket for my phone throughout the day. It's hard to disengage. Here's my checklist of where and when to detox from technology.

Instead of sleeping with your phone within reach, charge it overnight across the room from your bed. Once the alarm on your phone sounds, turn it off and try not to engage with your phone for the first ten minutes of your morning. For bonus points, charge it outside the room altogether and get yourself a separate alarm clock.

At concerts or live performances where you are tempted to record footage, leave the phone behind—or promise yourself it will only be one or two videos. Trust that experiencing it IRL is better than through a screen.

Leave your phone in the car if you're eating out. If you're eating at home, with family or alone, tuck it in a drawer or put it in a room away from the kitchen and dining room. Both Tan and Bobby refrain from pulling out their phone when they're dining with their husbands. (You may have noticed that the Fab Five spend a lot of time commenting on each other's Instagram posts, but I promise you it's never during dinnertime.)

PRE-GAME FOR TOUGH STUFF

Every day, we're faced with challenging situations. That's just what happens when 7.3 billion humans share a planet. (And with our country so divided right now, there are more challenges than ever before.) But each difficult encounter is a shot to learn and to come together with others. As soon as you initiate a conversation that gets you and someone else talking, you two are working together. If we're not talking to each other, we're not growing. But before you start that dialogue, be sure you can answer these three questions for yourself:

- *How do I hope this conversation will help me grow?*
- *How do I hope this conversation will help the other person grow?*
- *Do I know how to be responsive and not reactive?*

Once you can answer those questions, it's time for the following tactics.

ALWAYS INITIATE A TOUGH CONVO WITH SINCERE CURIOSITY. Ask why something is happening instead of making an accusation. The idea is that you want to lean in and learn why the other person is behaving a certain way that doesn't work for you.

DON'T THINK ABOUT YOUR CLAPBACKS. You may have even rehearsed a few of them, but this is not the place for sassy retorts. If you instigate a challenging talk, your job is to listen and let the other person respond without interference.

ALWAYS BE DIRECT. Don't try to lure someone into a difficult conversation or bring up a conflict midway into a friendly chat at the water cooler.

DON'T CONFRONT SOMEONE IN A PUBLIC SPACE. Talking within earshot of others will only color your responses and air personal business. Find a quiet neutral space like an empty conference room at work, or a shared space like a living room in your home that's not being used by others.

ANTICIPATE A RESOLUTION BEFORE YOU BEGIN TALKING. What I mean is you should be positive about the outcome so you operate with that goal in mind. If you imagine that a tough conversation will end in a bigger battle, you probably won't be respectful or allow yourself to be vulnerable. And that's how we connect and resolve issues.

On the flip side, if someone initiates a difficult conversation with you and you're not ready to engage or don't feel comfortable with the discussion, don't try to deftly shift the subject. Remember, be direct: Tell the other person that the conversation is making you uncomfortable and that you want to change the dialogue. If the other person can't honor your request, politely let that person know his or her lack of respect is not okay with you and walk away.

PRAISE YOU LIKE
I SHOULD

Would you believe that compliments and orgasms have a lot in common? Seriously, Swiss research has shown that receiving a compliment triggers the same response in your brain as a terrific toss between the sheets. The more specific and sincere the flattery you give, the bigger the mental pleasure payoff the other person gets. Another study, out of the University of Tokyo, revealed that getting a compliment related to a certain skill actually makes you perform better at it. That's almost as powerful of an incentive as receiving a cash reward.

Do you need any more reason to start dishing out some sincere praise? Well, here's one more. As a boy growing up in Missouri, Bobby had a habit of complimenting the waitress whenever his family went out to dinner. "I had my little country bumpkin accent and I would smile and say, 'I sure like your earrings,'" says Bobby. "I still do it because that compliment lets people know that you see them—and that you're not just looking past them."

The art of giving a great compliment is to focus the flattery on what's relevant. You wouldn't compliment a coworker on her shoes after she gave an impressive presentation. Tell her she killed it in the boardroom. If you see a dad struggling to teach his daughter a lesson about sharing, remark on his parenting skills, not his fly sunglasses. Of course, everyone *does* love to hear they look fantastic, too. Tan likes to pinpoint one aspect of someone's style when he gives a compliment. So instead of saying "You look amazing," he would smile and note, "That shade of green really brings out your eyes."

It's equally important to receive a compliment like a pro. My advice is to basically own it. We tend to deflect compliments, and that's because we don't believe we deserve them. That's a self-esteem issue. Allow someone's compliment to interrupt those negative thoughts in your mind and change your inner dialogue. Instead of denying generous praise, simply smile wide and say, "Thank you." No need to qualify why you did a great job or explain how you got your hair to look so smooth or where you got the shirt. A simple "thanks" and a smile will do.

One last thing: Returning the favor by giving a compliment back is just as important. There are a lot of people pleasers in the world who make it a point to validate others, but don't get that same validation for themselves. If someone gives you a sincere compliment, you don't have to do the same right away. It might come across as insincere. If you have a genuine compliment to give in return, wait a day or two and then give that person his or her own mental orgasm.

HIP TIP *For an instant posture correction, cross your left arm across your stomach and then place your right arm's elbow on the wrist. Then place the fist of your right arm under your chin.*

Often, we think of an apology as a way of mending fences, but that's not accurate. An apology is an acknowledgment of an act that has hurt someone else. Admitting a fault is never easy, but believe it or not, it's also not always appropriate. Before you apologize, ask yourself if doing so serves the other person. Many times, we dole out apologies to make ourselves feel better, but the point of an apology is to make sure the other person gets the closure he or she needs. So take a moment to think about whose ego you're serving when you offer up that amends. Also, be clear in your mind how that apology is going to help the other person get that closure.

To realize how your apology will affect another, take a moment to think about what the other person needs. Did you mistakenly neglect to include someone in a social plan and her pride is hurt? Your apology should restore her self-esteem by assuring her it was an oversight. Did you insult someone in a heated moment? Be sure to tell him you spoke out of anger and not from your heart. If you don't know how your apology can help, it's best to ask the person you plan to approach before you offer one. Allow the person to clearly express the closure he or she needs and then find the strength in yourself to make sure your apology is speaking directly to what that person has asked for.

The same goes for rebuilding burned bridges. You need to understand why you want this relationship to be repaired. You also have to understand that the legs this bridge was built on have all been broken and must be rebuilt with new pillars of trust and understanding. Apologies and building bridges are all about being clear in your intention and making sure that your actions serve a specific need.

One more thing. Don't overapologize. If you know you didn't do something wrong, there's no need to admit wrongdoing. Of course, there are a handful of occasions where you just might have to bite the bullet and do it—like in an email to your boss—but as a general rule, if you don't have anything to be sorry for, don't be sorry.

HIP TIP

To help remember someone's name, use it as soon as you hear it. If you meet a "Karamo," repeat it back to him in conversation by saying something like, "Nice bomber jacket, Karamo."

Karamo and . . . Jonathan's legs and heels.

IT'S NOT ABOUT WHAT OTHER PEOPLE WILL THINK, AND IT'S NOT ABOUT SOMEONE ELSE'S EXPECTATIONS OF YOU. GO AFTER WHAT YOU WANT IN LIFE BECAUSE THAT SUCCESS WILL MAKE *YOU* HAPPY AT THE END OF THE DAY.

—KARAMO

HIP TIP *To reach a goal, don't get overwhelmed by the scale of your objective. Start small, and each minor accomplishment will add up to a major achievement.*

THE FIRST IMPRESSION

A first date and a job interview are a lot alike. Basically, you're meeting someone to see if you connect in a way that could lead to a long-term, emotionally lucrative relationship. Now, would you meet a prospective employer late at night while doing a body shot at a loud, noisy club? (If you're nodding right now, I would love to hear more about what you do for a living.) Probably not your long-term romantic partner, either. Here are my tips for where, when, and how to plan a first networking meeting or date that leads to something more meaningful than a hangover.

DON'T: Go to places that are loud. That includes bars, clubs, and raging parties. You get my drift. Even meeting with someone about a job opening at a noisy, bustling restaurant can be distracting and make you appear unfocused.

TRY THIS: Pick a setting that allows you to soak up some culture, like an art gallery or a museum exhibition, and then use that inspiration as a preliminary talking point. It makes sense, for example, to meet at a fashion show if you're connecting with a colleague who works for a clothing designer.

DO: Talk about your strengths in terms of how they apply to a relationship or job position. For instance, elaborating on your loyal nature makes sense on a first date; likewise, stressing that you're a collaborative team player is what an employer wants to hear.

DON'T: The same applies to venues where you need to be silent. That would be, for example, movies, operas or plays, or churches. First dates are all about communication.

DON'T: Ask yes-or-no questions. A conversation doesn't go anywhere if someone simply affirms or negates a statement.

TRY THIS: Acknowledge your weaknesses if someone asks you to reveal a few of them. (Employers are particularly known for this line of questioning.) Just be sure to frame them as flaws you're working on.

DO: Show off your confidence by sitting up straight, making direct eye contact, and genuinely smiling with ease. Jonathan wants me to add here that proper personal grooming—combed, clean hair, say, and flossed teeth—says that you take care of yourself because you know you're worth it.

DO: Listen closely to details. This is your time to assess whether you're compatible with a person or a position. If you're on a date, is your date someone who hates the beach and you're an avid surfer? When you're talking business, the fine print of a job is critical. Does this new gig call for monthly travel and you're a new parent or someone who has just adopted a puppy?

DO: Make a point to connect on an issue or preference by relating something the other person says back to yourself. For instance, if he or she says, "I grew up on a ranch," talk about how you love riding horses—if that's true, of course. Now you're having a shared dialogue.

DO: Make inquiries that begin with "what" or "why" or "how." Deeper questions— like "What made you decide to study journalism?" or "How did you find the time to get two degrees?"—provoke deeper responses.

DO: Tackle one big issue. Meaning, you can ask a potential partner, "Why did your last relationship end?" or "What was your childhood like?" On a job interview, it's perfectly appropriate to ask about annual earnings or job security. A lot of times, we like to keep these first conversations superficial, but the whole reason you're on a date or in an interview is to get closer on a profound level. Just be sure to limit it to one—don't stay stuck in reflective mode.

Your social media impact matters. Have fun and be your true authentic self.

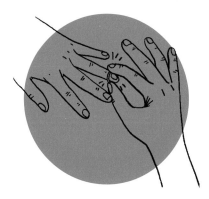

The first time I met my fiancé, TV director Ian Jordan, I swept him off his feet—literally. I saw him standing outside a club in West Hollywood and knew that I wanted to get to know him better. Or at least, make an unforgettable impression. So I snuck up behind him and hoisted him up in the air. How's that for playing it cool? (Don't worry, we had been eyeing each other, so it wasn't like I accosted him out of nowhere.) Cut to eight happy years later and it was time to take our commitment to the next level. In other words, one of us needed to propose.

In the end, I asked Ian to marry me in a big, bold way (hold on, I'll get to that story), and that night will always be part of our story. Here are some questions to ask yourself before you commit to someone on a profound level—whether you propose or not. After all, saying "I do" is the easy part.

WHY: Do you want to stay with this person or get married because all of your friends have tied the knot? You should be motivated by an overwhelming desire to spend the rest of your life with this person. I knew Ian was the man for me on that first night I met him. That feeling never subsided— and still hasn't.

WHO: Make sure you know this person's life values and long-term goals—and that what he or she wants works with your views and future plans. Ian and I have what I call "check-in" dinners where we talk about what we want to achieve *together* and make sure we're on the same page.

WHEN: Four years into our relationship, Ian and I discussed the idea of marriage. It took us another four years to get engaged, but by that time we both knew we wanted to spend our lives together. There is no right or wrong amount of dating time that should precede a further commitment. Don't succumb to any pressure from family or friends. Pop the question when it feels right to you.

HOW: Whether you take a knee and ask for someone's hand at sunset or have a jumbotron do the honors at a World Series game, your proposal should reflect *both* of you, meaning don't pop the question at Disneyland if your partner gets nauseous on amusement park rides. Tan and his husband, Rob, proposed to each other in a conversation. One day Rob said to Tan, "I'd marry you in a heartbeat." Tan replied, "Me too. We should get married one day. That sounds lovely." A few years later, they tied the knot in a low-key ceremony. For Ian, I planned a sur-prise birthday-engagement party in L.A. with all of our friends and family on hand—after first asking his mom for permission. When I got down to propose, I told him why he was the one before I asked him to marry me: "You are the funniest man I know, the kindest man, my biggest cheerleader. You made me feel like I could do anything."

ASK ME ANYTHING

I wanted to do an FAQ section here to cover some of the things that plague people most frequently. Also, because I want you to know I'm an open book and I'm here for you no matter what you want to talk about.

My family fights about politics every holiday and someone inevitably storms out. Then, the food gets cold. How can we come together? You already know why it's not working. You just said it: You're fighting—not having conversations. The keys to engaging in a real conversation are respect and listening. That doesn't mean you have to agree, but it does mean you have to respect that we all have different points of view—and be willing to really hear someone else's POV, too. Lastly, if you feel the conversation is getting heated, ask, "Are we still listening to each other and respecting each other?" If the answer is no, stop the conversation. (Also remember that one vote doesn't define a person. It only shows where that person is at that moment in his or her life.) *You can apply this same approach to a casual work lunch, drinks with old friends, or any context where conversations turn into fights.*

I'm stuck in a rut at my job. Is there a way to make it exciting again? Question for you: Is this job your dream or is it a paycheck? If this job is your dream, then yes, you can get out of the rut. Spend time remembering the passion that got you into this position. Interact with coworkers that have that same passion and share ideas with them. If this job is just a paycheck, then you need to start taking the steps to go after your dream, beginning by figuring out what that dream is. *You can ask similar questions about your most important personal relationships, particularly the one with a significant other.*

What do I say to my coworker who just lost his wife to cancer? You don't need to say anything beyond "I'm so sorry for your loss." Be open to having the other person share with you the loving memories they have of the person they just lost, but only when he or she is ready to. Let someone who's grieving do all the talking. Give him or her an opportunity to focus on the good moments, the happy moments, and the loving moments shared with the loved one who has passed. Lastly, remind that person that no one should rush the healing process. He or she can and should heal at his or her own pace. *You can apply this same approach to any situation that involves a setback, like a friend getting let go from a job.*

Public speaking terrifies me, and I have to make a toast at my sister's wedding. Any tips? What is it that scares you most about public speaking—is it the people, the attention, the speech? You need to first identify where the fear is coming from. Practice your toast in the mirror and in front of close friends. Be sure it has a beginning, middle, and end like any good story. If you still can't get past the fear, invite a buddy to co-toast with you. That way, you will have onstage someone who you can play off of and who can support you as you speak. *You can also use this exercise if you're nervous about making a presentation at work or even a sales pitch. You can invite a coworker to help you with visuals so you won't feel solely in the spotlight.*

I say "sorry" all the time to make my friends feel better, but one of them says I should stop apologizing so much. Whose side are you on? If you didn't do anything wrong, why are you so sorry? Apologies are meant for when your actions directly hurt someone else. If you haven't done anything wrong, don't say "sorry"—you're assigning blame to yourself for no reason. If you have done something wrong, acknowledge it and then quickly state how you will correct your behavior from here on out. *This note applies to every area of your life.*

My boyfriend shuts down whenever I want to talk about our relationship. How can I get him to listen so we can get closer? Don't bring too many issues to the conversation. Every journey starts with one step, but for some reason we want to get it all out while we're communicating. That's because we live in a culture where information moves so fast. So when you're talking to your partner, make sure you focus on one issue even though you may have a list of five things to discuss. Don't let it bleed into number two or number four. *Use this logic when you're talking to a colleague or your boss, too.*

> **HIP TIP** *Be punctual by always planning to arrive ten minutes early for a lunch date or a meeting. Being on time shows that you value that person's time as much as your own.*

HOW TO TALK TRANS

The culture of gender identity has evolved at lightning speed in the last decade. But the etiquette can be confusing—even for this proud, informed gay man. These pointers are borrowed from GLAAD, a media advocacy group for the LGBTQ (lesbian, gay, bisexual, transgender, questioning or queer) community. The more you know, the better you can relate to people around you.

Don't make assumptions about a transgender person's sexual orientation.

Don't ask a transgender person what their "real name" is.

Be careful about disclosure, confidentiality, and "outing."

Respect the terminology a transgender person uses to describe their identity.

Be patient with a person who is questioning or exploring their gender identity.

Five-Minute Make-Better: What's Your Mantra?

The Sanskrit word *mantra* means, in its essence, a sacred saying with mystical power. For me, a personal mantra is more of a life mindset that cuts through self-doubt or distraction. To create your own personal mantra, think about a saying that gives you strength or encourages you to be brave or kind. Just be sure it's positive and easy to repeat when you look in the mirror in the morning.

My boys and I want to share our mantras with you:

KARAMO

BE NOT AFRAID OF GOING SLOWLY; BE AFRAID ONLY OF STANDING STILL.

It reminds me that taking small steps is fine, as long as I am moving forward toward a goal.

JONATHAN

IT'S OKAY TO SAY NO AND NOT EXPLAIN WHY.

I have a huge people-pleaser part in me that has always exhausted me.

TAN

LEARN IT ALL. DO IT ALL.

Everything in my life that I have done has come from learning more than I'd expected would be necessary. It empowers you.

BOBBY

NEVER TAKE NO FOR AN ANSWER.

That may have to be engraved on my tombstone.

ANTONI

I'M PERFECT JUST THE WAY I AM.

I cringe and get goose bumps when I say it because I'm like, "No, I'm not." I have to remind myself to say it with pride.

HOUSE RULES

Create a chic, functional home that makes you happy every day

**O**n *Queer Eye*, I have just three days to completely transform a living room or a kitchen or even most of a house. But let's get something straight: Renovations like that don't just begin, end, and happen—especially when you're talking about a space that hasn't been updated since *The Golden Girls* went into syndication.

That's the magic of television and the craziness of our schedule on the show. We have exactly seventy-two hours to transform our heroes' lives. Okay, so I do get some time to familiarize myself with the hero's lifestyle before that clock starts, but really, the heavy lifting happens so quickly because I have the support of an amazing construction team. (But when I say seventy-two hours, I mean it—sometimes we're even working through the night!) When people come up to me and ask why they don't see as much of me on the show as the other boys, I laugh and say, "Honey, that's because I'm off building a wall unit or repainting a vintage dresser."

The reality of remodeling, redecorating, or even just swapping out furniture for a few new pieces is that it has to be a thoughtful process. You don't want to be impulsive, because these decisions make a huge impact on how you live, day to day. Most of the time, home design miscalculations are difficult and costly to reverse. As an interior designer, I always tell my clients to really think about their needs before they start admiring beautiful fabric swatches or rolling around on floor model mattresses. Who doesn't love to test mattresses? Thankfully, *unlike* me, you don't need to settle on anything overnight—and you shouldn't. Returning a beautiful bouclé camelback sofa because it can't be shimmied through your front door can run you hundreds of dollars. Trust

me, I have seen this sort of thing happen dozens of times, and going back to square one can be extremely frustrating, to say the least.

I also stress thinking long and hard about décor because what you surround yourself with spills into other areas of your life and impacts your daily routines. If you love your new dining room, you're more likely to throw a dinner party and maybe even host your fussy in-laws for Thanksgiving this year. (Who needs more wine?) If your kitchen has the right appliances and enough counter space, you'll be inspired to cook more often and more inventively. As for the bedroom, which is actually where you spend most of your life, a tranquil setting makes for better shut-eye—not to mention, more action between those new Egyptian cotton sheets.

You might assume I live in a perfect, painstakingly organized home with sleek furniture and every throw cushion in place. Nope. I'm actually glaring at a coffee table strewn with keys, mail, and remote controls right now. No matter how many times Dewey and I redesign our home, there will always be closets crammed with our excess outerwear and kitchen drawers brimming with receipts, scattered change, and even a misplaced bow tie. (I've been looking for that!) We have an ongoing battle about why I shove clutter in drawers and closets when we're expecting company. I say, "Because I want our home to be warm and inviting."

But the bottom line is that life can be messy. That's all the more reason to make your home a warm, peaceful sanctuary that awaits you after a long day. When you wake up in the morning and you can breathe better because you're not overwhelmed by the chaos of your home, the rest of the world feels a whole lot less chaotic. Just remember that what we do on *Queer Eye* is pretty extreme. You probably won't need a construction crew to create a space you love. But hey, I get it if you really want to borrow my hard hat.

Give a fluffed throw pillow a quick chop to make your sofa or bed look neat and tidy.

Before I tackle any redesign project, the very first thing I do is sit down with clients in their space and ask them three simple, straightforward questions. The goal here is to figure out the best plan to make your home more practical, comfortable, and desirable. In essence, let's create a dwelling that works for your particular needs and that you absolutely love.

NUMBER 1: *How is this room going to function?* Will your fancy new dining room be the go-to space for every meal? Or will you eat in front of the TV more often— no judgment!—and use the dining room exclusively for dinner parties?

If it's the former, I know this space stands to get lots of foot traffic and calls for durable fabric on the chairs and a sturdy table that doesn't scratch easily. If it's the latter, you can opt for less practical pieces, like a glossy, lacquered dining table and formal, upholstered dining room chairs. Once you decide how a room will be used, you can fill in the elements around its function.

NUMBER 2: *How many people will be using this room?* Then, do the math. That head count tells you whether you need a standard sofa for three or a huge sectional for six in a living room. Or how many face towels to buy for a bathroom. It also dictates everything from the size of a kitchen table to the amount of refrigerator storage space you'll need.

NUMBER 3: *What is your daily routine?* Are you someone like Jonathan who loves to soak in a bath every night, surrounded by candlelight? In that case, you'll want to factor in a sizable spa tub. Or maybe you're a culinary whiz like Antoni and prefer to focus on a gourmet stovetop and oven.

Take a moment to ask yourself these questions in any space you want to beautify. Sit down in each room for a few minutes, look around, and soak up how you feel in that area before you jot down whatever comes to mind. Be sure to use a dedicated pad (or folder on your computer or even note on your iPhone) that you will refer to for all of your home improvements going forward. You don't want to misplace scraps of paper with square footage measurements or other important notes.

Before you say, "Bobby, I'm thinking Danish modern meets Spanish revival," we need to bring up budget. You can't imagine how many people swan dive into a home project before estimating how much they're going to spend—or at least how much they'd like to spend! Whether you're remodeling a bathroom or buying a new sofa, that magic number will affect so many decisions. As an interior designer, I bring up money early on with my clients. If they haven't decided on a number, I have to table the project until they do. If you work with a pro on any home improvements or go it alone, that discussion needs to happen—maybe just with yourself—before you start poring over club chairs on Pinterest.

Obviously, the cost of a redo varies wildly according to taste, size, materials, and other details. But there are some rough guidelines that can help you in the planning process. For instance, a kitchen remodel can span anywhere from $4,500 for a smaller space to well over $50,000 for an upscale overhaul, but the national average comes in at about $20,500. A bathroom—again, these are estimates—runs between $6,000 and $14,000. Those are the two rooms that most people choose to overhaul. A living room or den redo is where you spend the bulk of your budget on new furniture because you need the most seating and tables in there. And it's worth it, because that's probably where you spend a lot of your time, both alone and with guests.

Figuring out a budget takes a few steps. First, create an "I Wish List" that covers your home design upgrade. Don't even consider money at this point because this lineup is simply a way to get a sense of your dreams. Next, take a serious look at your finances and see how much you can realistically allocate to redecorating or to a full rehab. One popular rule of thumb is to annually set aside 1 percent of the purchase price of your home to channel into annual improvements. (So if you paid $500,000 for your home, you're looking at spending $5,000 each year on upgrades.) Assuming you can afford it, you should consider doubling or tripling that amount for a renovation project if you haven't sunk any money into your home in the past few years. Remember that many renovations, like a new kitchen or master bathroom, add value to your home. I always remind people that more superficial tweaks like redecorating add more value to your life.

Renting? Don't make any major structural changes for obvious reasons. Instead, set aside money in a fund for when you do buy your own place. I moved around a lot in my twenties, so I know what it's like to live transitionally but still want to imprint your taste on a leased space. It's totally doable. See my tips on how to make a rental feel more personal on page 185.

Now start researching and comparison shopping to see if your wish list lines up with your budget. If you're in the market for a new sofa, look online at different designs that match your price range and then visit stores to lounge on your top three picks. Itching to redo your bathroom? Contact a few local contractors to get bids on how much a project of your desired scope will cost. I always ask for the high- and low-end options on materials like fixtures, tile, or flooring. That way, you can choose what you want to splurge on, like hand-glazed tiles or a shower for two.

No matter your budget, the world of home design has never been more accessible and affordable. Between online resources and affordable emporiums, there are myriad options and price points. Lots of my sky's-the-limit clients blend custom pieces with mass-market finds.

BAUHAUS VS. BAROQUE

Deciding on a decorating style can be daunting. Should you go with a mid-century modern look? Or boho? And what the hell is rococo, you ask? (It's a really ornate style from the eighteenth century, just so you know. I'm not a fan.) Instead of trying to school yourself in centuries of design history, think above all about creating a joyful space. That's what we all want: a house that makes us smile and sigh with happiness as soon as we walk in the door.

Sure, you could appoint your entire living room with sleek Scandinavian pieces and make it resemble a designer showroom. But do you want to come home to a formal setup every night that's more reflective of a décor magazine cover than your personal taste? I would much rather create a setting that embodies who I am. Tan and I agree that trends, whether in fashion or home design, shouldn't be anyone's prevailing personal reference.

First of all, design fads fade, so you could be making decisions based on style cues that will be passé in a few years. (And furniture is even harder to replace than clothes—trust me.) Secondly, the home design industry needs to make profits. That's, in part, why they change

up what's "hot" seasonally to encourage you to redo your home. If you base your choices on what you adore rather than what's "on trend," you won't run the risk of falling out of love with your new living room or kitchen.

To get a sense of which style works for you, create a vision board that includes absolutely anything you love, whether it's home-related or not. One of your items could be a cozy sweater, a textured painting, a cool building, or even a colorful pool float. (Yes, you read that right. I have used a pool toy as inspiration.) With this approach, you get a distinct sense of what will make you happy without trying to determine if you dig the clean lines of modernist design or the voluptuous curves of the shabby chic look.

Here's a great example of how inspiration is every-where: Recently, I was walking by an old, faded pink building in downtown Los Angeles at the end of the day. The sunset was hitting the face of it just perfectly and accentuating the patina of that distressed pink. "Wow," I thought. "That's the exact shade I've been looking for to repaint my office." So I snapped a picture on my phone and a paint shop color matched the hue, which is now the color of my office.

Once you have a vision board that captures your style, refer to it when you shop online or in stores. It can be pretty simple to translate the clues you collected. For instance, if you included a big, soft sweater, look to ample, comfortable pieces like swivel club chairs or sectional sofas that envelop you, rather than wood furniture with minimal padding. Your love for a textured painting reveals that you're drawn to depth in design, so look for woven fabrics with interesting patterns on chairs or in window treatments; you can also create that depth and dimension with wallpaper or rugs with geometric motifs. One hero

on *Queer Eye* told me that his favorite series was *Mad Men* (Don Draper was his style icon, naturally) and his dream vacation was to visit Cuba. To mirror his passions in a design scheme, I combined the sleek qualities of design during the *Mad Men* period (the sixties) with the bright, dynamic colors you see in Havana.

Wait. What about the pool float? Ha. I knew you'd ask. The float's vivid colors inspired that client to pick out a sculptural coral-hued sofa that popped in the den.

HIP TIP *Whether you're a "no shoes" household or not, a chic bench with hidden storage eliminates scattered discarded footwear by the entrance of your home.*

RENT (NOT THE MUSICAL)

A few quick ideas for easily and affordably making a temporary space feel more like a permanent home:

If you have no outdoor space, create an **indoor herb garden** that brings bright foliage and seasonings to your kitchen.

Use temporary, **removable wallpaper** to enliven the wall behind your bed or to welcome guests in a foyer.

Mount art on bookshelves or even a **stepladder** instead of hanging pictures with nails.

Replace a dated or unsightly chandelier or sconces with chic, **new fixtures,** as lighting can easily be installed and taken down.

A HAPPY HOME CAN GIVE YOU A WHOLE NEW OUTLOOK ON LIFE. WHEN YOU WAKE UP AND EVERYTHING IS IN ORDER, THE WORLD DOESN'T FEEL SO UNMANAGEABLE. YOU WALK OUT THE DOOR FEELING CALM AND CONFIDENT.

—BOBBY

HIP TIP *Make the front door the star of your home. In Palm Springs, for instance, where most of the houses are very streamlined, you see vivid red, canary-yellow, and azure-blue doors that pop.*

Behold the coffee table, the focal point of most living rooms—and not just because it's where you keep the remote. This hardworking, low-slung piece of furniture is the perfect place to showcase your personal taste in art books, flowers, and artifacts. I like to vary the height of the displayed items and create a striking and harmonious composition. Bowls, busts, vases, and candles work nicely, too. (You can take these notes when styling your shelves, as well.) While you're at it, stow away that remote in a lidded leather or ceramic box to complete the elegant look. Or look for a table with built-in storage like drawers or shelves underneath. To avoid putting your feet up on the table—a hard-to-break habit, I admit—add a few ottomans underneath. Antoni and his boyfriend have vintage Omersa leather animal footstools in their living room.

Shortcuts to Design Style You don't have to leave your house to find even more indicators of your personal preferences. Tan taught you that your clothes speak volumes about your taste. Use that know-how in your home. If you love peasant blouses inspired by the seventies, look to bohemian styles in design. Got five nautical shirts and two pairs of boat shoes? Think coastal accents. Tan loves to change up his look and mix contemporary fashion with vintage pieces, so his 1906 Tudor in Salt Lake City reflects his eclecticism. He says: "I mix different periods and styles like mid-century modern with country French. I don't really care if I'm breaking any rules."

Your taste in pop culture like music and movies and books converts to valuable style references, too. "I love everything to be aged with cracks and scuffs so it has a story," says Antoni, whose apartment pays homage to the organic curves and free-form shapes employed by design pioneers like Milo Baughman of the sixties. It's no surprise that his favorite films include *Blow-Up* and *The Graduate*, both from that decade, too.

HIP TIP *If you own your space, modernize dated appliances with enamel paint that dries glossy in a fun, unpredictable shade like green apple or bright orange.*

THE HIGHS & LOWS

Sink the bulk of your budget into rooms where you spend the most time. But when it comes to essential design needs, here are my thoughts on where to splurge and to save.

BREAK THE PIGGY BANK

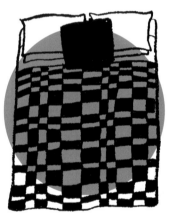

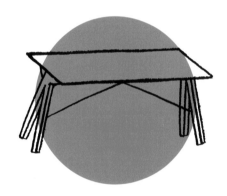

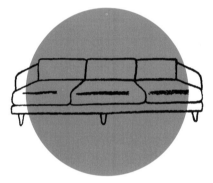

BEDDING: Even when I had the crappiest apartment in all of New York City, I spent good money on my sheets. But don't buy into what I call "the thread count conspiracy." That's just a marketing ploy. The amount of threads has nothing to do with comfort; it's the length of the fiber and the quality of the fabric that makes it baby-bottom soft or unbearably scratchy. Look for Egyptian cotton with long-staple fibers (the staple simply refers to the length). Personally, I think it's more comfortable and polished than sateen with its silky sheen, or durable percale cotton, or the unmistakably rumpled look of linen.

DINING ROOM TABLE: Your guests may not notice your dishes, but they will most certainly judge an unstable table. Check for solid construction—nicks or scratches on a floor sample are bad omens—and be sure it seats double the number of your family members (each place setting calls for twenty-two to twenty-four inches). Opt for dark fabrics if you're going with upholstered dining room chairs—I have seen new white linen chairs get murdered by Cabernet stains.

SOFA: Sturdy hardwood frames are the way to go; low-cost pine or particleboard could warp after a few years. I always avoid a sofa with a long, single seat cushion, because usually we grow accustomed to sitting in the same spot, and it will start to sag. It's better to be able to move the cushions around. When it comes to fabric, I recommend polyester blends over cottons and velvets, which show wear and are tougher to spot clean.

CUT A FEW CORNERS

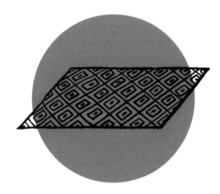

WINDOW TREATMENTS: Custom window treatments can cost up to $20,000 for one room—which, unless you're obsessed with a certain designer fabric or plan to stay in your home for years to come, doesn't seem necessary. Instead, opt for readymade panels and hardware that can be hung and swapped out when you change up your décor.

RUG: Hello, you're literally walking all over it! The issue with synthetic material rugs and natural fiber versions made from jute or sisal is that they can shed for years. Avoid that pesky dilemma with affordable felted wool, which is my preference. It wears well and adds texture to a room. Be sure to rotate your rug every six months so it will wear evenly.

THROW PILLOWS: Rather than go custom with cushions, you can find a great selection of these accents at great prices. I prefer to go with three or four pillows in varying sizes, but make sure they don't exceed the back of your sofa in height—that looks sloppy. Since colors and prints can clash easily, I like to liven up a monochromatic palette with texture and slight variations of one neutral color like ecru or camel.

BE BOLD

Nothing says sophistication like vibrant walls. But your space should never shriek, "Look at me! Love me!" Way too desperate. Still, it's easy to overdo it with a heady hue when you're making a big decision based on a tiny paint chip. If you want to make a statement with color but are unsure of where to start, I recommend these three bold but balanced shades.

TERRA COTTA

Look for: A lot of people think of this Latin name for "baked earth" more as a pottery material than a paint possibility. But the right color can instantly add warmth and the rustic vibe of a Tuscan villa, especially when you pair it with raw wood.

Look away: Shades dominated by too much pink or taupe can come off like a cartoon sunset. And bypass anything that resembles rust, for obvious reasons.

NAVY BLUE

Look for: I love a dark, rich—even near black—maritime blue with a touch of gray that adds depth or dimension. Pair it with white trim for a pop of contrast.

Look away: Be sure to veer from hues with violet undertones, which will read purple in a lot of light, or royal tones that could come off too bright and juvenile.

LEAF GREEN

Look for: Think soothing forest, not margarita. The right, classic warm green— one that you would see outside—echoes nature and makes any room feel oasis-like.

Look away: Avoid any neon-ish shade with a lot of yellow. That will read retro in a "sad motel diner on Route 66" way.

HIP TIP *A blah dining room table gets a facelift when you paint the legs a different color from the top of the table. Or switch the focus and paint just the top. Either way, the final effect looks custom.*

LIVING LARGER

Most of us—including this city dweller—don't live in palatial homes with infinite square footage and ceilings that graze the clouds. We contend with modest living spaces, cramped closets, and cluttered kitchens. But don't feel confined by those four walls or stubby ceilings. Here are my tried-and-true tips for making a room look almost twice its size.

CHEAT THE EYE. Floor-to-ceiling bookshelves or paneling that goes three-quarters of the way up a wall draws the eye skyward and visually expands a space. Increase that illusion with a tonal and monochromatic palette of books and curios.

HOIST IT HIGH. Anchoring curtains right at the top of your window frames is a lost opportunity. Instead, extend the rod about a foot above the window frame and be sure it exceeds the width on either side. Your window instantly appears larger and opens up your space. Voilà!

GET LIT. By creating "layers" of lighting with multiple sources like table lamps and ceiling fixtures, you encourage the eye to bounce around a space, making it seem more expansive.

GO LEGGY. Just like sexy stilettos elongate a silhouette, adding legs to furniture heightens its shape, brings it off the floor, and creates a visual line beneath it. Now your room looks airier.

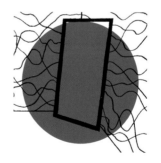

SEE DOUBLE. A large mirror—whether you hang it or artfully lean it in a corner—tricks us into seeing space twice its size. I love a massive full-length in a dining room or bedroom corner.

GO GREEN

Forget the simple fact that houseplants add color and bring nature indoors. They're also important to your well-being. A simple spider plant or succulent releases oxygen and literally removes air toxins so you can breathe better. Studies have shown that indoor plants also reduce stress and boost productivity. How's that for hardworking? In my space, we have a few cacti ❶ and a ficus tree ❷. You'll always find a vibrant orchid ❸ on our coffee table as well. Antoni describes his Brooklyn apartment as a "man jungle" with a massive, ten-foot-tall fiddle-leaf fig tree ❹, two huge banana trees ❺, and a couple of bird-of-paradise plants ❻.

A grouping of plants in a corner with a comfortable armchair or a settee nearby creates an indoor sanctuary. This little nook can be a perfect place to meditate or curl up with a book. Not only do you get to relax amid nature, but caring for plants can also be therapeutic. Seeing a plant thrive or maybe even bloom makes you feel like a good nurturer. For me, just misting the orchid blossoms at the end of the day is part of my daily wind-down ritual.

To go green, take measurements of any rooms that you plan to adorn with foliage (don't forget the height of the ceilings if you're considering trees) and make note of the amount of sun your space receives throughout the day. Then, visit a local nursery and ask a specialist to assist you in creating an indoor garden, or even just picking out one plant.

When you decorate with your new greenery, think outside of the traditional pot or planter. Vintage brass and ceramic pots make a bold statement, and the same goes for a cool coffee or imported tomato can. Spruce up bookshelves, entry tables, fireplace mantels, staircase corners or landings, and ample bathtub rims with your new potted friends.

MY EX WUZ HERE

Sex with an ex is one thing. However, a bed, especially a duvet cover you shared with a former lover, has no place in a new relationship. Karamo confirms that being surrounded by items strongly associated with a previous relationship makes it harder to let go, even if you don't realize that you're still hanging on. I'm all about energy and flow, so I usually advise a ceremonial purge of items left over from a previous affair—barring pets, of course. Fido can stay. Stay, Fido.

Here's what has to go:

Bedding This is non-negotiable, and considering that we spend 30 percent of our lives in bed, you're probably due for an upgrade anyway.

Mementos Framed photos of you and Mr. Not Right Now in front of the Eiffel Tower? That's a no-brainer. But even a picture taken by an ex can trigger memories. Ditto for cutesy knickknacks or even pieces of art with a backstory. If there's some ephemera that makes you think of an ex every time you see it, remove it from display. Karamo recommends that you unload these pieces online or at a yard sale and use the funds to shop for new accents.

Personal items Clear out his side of the medicine cabinet—including any grooming tools and prescription bottles.

Let's talk about porn. More specifically, food porn. Everywhere you look, from social media to magazines to the countless cooking shows on TV, there are images of perfectly composed dishes. Friends post plates of avocado toast wearing watermelon radish bikinis on Instagram. You see cakes on baking shows that are ten feet tall with tiers enrobed in twenty-four-karat gold glitter. Who can forget the frenzy caused by the online exposure of the Cronut?

Don't get me wrong. This attention to food makes me a happy guy. I love that people care so much about food. Anyone will tell you that I can wax passionately about a hunk of nutty, salty Gouda for hours. But these days, it seems we're all obsessed with looking at artful pictures of succulent roast chicken instead of making one—let alone tasting one. What a lost opportunity! People tell me that they never miss an episode of their favorite cooking show, but then admit in the same sentence that they rarely turn on their oven. That makes me sad because cooking, and eating, are such great pleasures. I want everyone to experience the thrill and confidence that comes with making a dish that delivers delicious bites.

You might not think of it this way, but food is truly self-care. Eating is one of the most important ways we honor our body. Starting your day with a healthy, mindful meal might be the only me time you get in your busy schedule. My morning ritual finds me making high-octane, black-as-tar coffee in my French press as soon as I wake up. As Jonathan

would say, I am "struggs to func" without my a.m. brew. Just grinding the dark roast beans (ah, that aroma) and pouring the steaming water over the coffee soothes me. No matter what happens when I walk out the door of my apartment, I'm better equipped to deal because of those few minutes I took for myself—and thanks to the caffeine coursing through my bloodstream, naturally.

Similarly, preparing a meal at the end of the day can be the perfect way to unwind. Chopping carrots for a stew or gently stirring a pot of simmering risotto is therapeutic. It forces you to focus on the task at hand instead of reflecting on some silly office gossip or the chores you neglected to cross off your to-do list. Plus, when you cook with a partner or kids, you're all on the same team, with a shared goal to get something delicious on the table.

But enough about you. Feeding someone else is a service. It's the ultimate act of love and care you can pass on to another person. So many of the heroes I meet on *Queer Eye* are looking for a way to show up for their friends and their families. Once they feel confident about making a pot of hearty turkey chili or a refreshing margarita, the first thing they want to do is share their newfound skill with people they cherish. (Aw, I might be getting a little teary-eyed just thinking about their big hearts.)

In this chapter, consider yourself my sous-chef. (No apron necessary—unless it's a super-cute one, of course.) We will outline your practical needs together, and I'll introduce you to some basic kitchen wisdom. No matter what your approach to eating may be, I want to make you fall in love with cooking. My goal is to get you excited about finding fresh ingredients, learning new and easy ways to create a fantastic meal in less than fifteen minutes, and tasting exotic spices. I want you to dance around the kitchen as you whisk eggs, and sing while you mince garlic. I bet you $20 that you will actually look forward to grocery shopping when you're done reading. Yes, I'm that confident.

Once you empower yourself in the kitchen, feeding yourself and others becomes fulfilling and fun. Hey, everybody has to eat. Let's enjoy every single bite.

IF THESE WALLS COULD TALK

As soon as I step into your kitchen, I get a good sense of your relationship with food. There are clues everywhere. Are your counters a showcase for gleaming appliances like a panini press, an espresso machine, or a food processor? (And if those gadgets are way too shiny, I can tell that you haven't touched them lately.) Does your gas stovetop look like it gets fired up regularly, or is that sad, battered, crumb-filled toaster oven doing all of your cooking? Just seeing what you have displayed tells me a lot about your skill level and interest in cooking.

Next, I crack open the fridge and assess the contents, or maybe the lack thereof. Yes, some people have literally nothing inside of their refrigerator except an expired jar of furry olives. (*Extra* dirty martini, anyone?) If that sounds familiar, you probably either have a jammed social calendar or every local take-out joint on speed dial. Others have stocked their refrigerator shelves and drawers with enough produce, dairy, and protein to weather a zombie apocalypse. If that's you, I would love to see your idea of a light lunch.

Do I peek in your drawers and open your kitchen cabinets, too? You bet I do. I want to analyze your arsenal of utensils and see whether or not you own a decent no-stick pan to cook a proper omelet. You may be able to flip a chicken breast with a fork in lieu of a spatula, but there are certain essential tools, spices, and staples required to cook even the most basic dishes. (I'll get to my checklists soon enough.)

But let's start here: Look around your kitchen and think about what it says about you and about how you approach eating. Pretend my boys and I just stormed into your house—what do you want us to learn when we look around? This is the room where both family and guests tend to congregate, so make sure it feels reflective of you.

CUTS LIKE A KNIFE

I love the tiny, humble kitchen in my Brooklyn apartment. But with only about 150 square feet to cook and maneuver in, I have to be a staunch minimalist. On the facing page are the ten essential tools every passionate home cook should own . . . knives and beyond.

CHEF'S KNIFE: This tool is your BFF in the kitchen. Choose one with an eight-inch razor-sharp blade and an ultra-comfortable grip. You'll turn to it to chop, dice, and mince veggies, and to cut through poultry and meat.

PARING KNIFE: Use this mini three-inch chef's knife with a sharp blade and tip to peel potatoes, thinly slice garlic, devein shrimp, and core tomatoes.

SERRATED BREAD KNIFE: Don't discount this dangerously sharp knife as if it's only for slicing a baguette. You'll use it to cut sandwiches, but also tomatoes, eggplants, and other soft veggies, without having to apply pressure and squish them.

MICROPLANE: Not just for grating zingy Parmesan, this tool replaces a garlic press (just run peeled cloves along the blade), shaves chocolate, zests citrus, and grates spices like whole nutmeg and cinnamon.

EIGHT-INCH COPPER POT: Though it's more expensive than stainless steel, copper conducts and retains heat evenly, so soups and sauces cook more uniformly in this medium pot. It looks beautiful on a stove, too, so I won't be mad if you leave it on top.

DUTCH OVEN: Consider this sturdy, enameled cast iron contraption with a lid your most self-sufficient vessel in the kitchen. It's perfect for making stew, chili, mussels, and even pounds of pasta. This workhorse can be left on the stove for hours, and it's safe to go in the oven as well.

CAST IRON SKILLET: This pan is a naturally nonstick, inexpensive, versatile wonder that sears meat because it goes to a higher heat than stainless steel cookware. It also goes from stovetop to oven in a snap for baking and broiling. Even better, you never wash it with soap, so the skillet retains the natural seasoning of everything you cook.

MEDIUM NONSTICK PAN: Eggs, pancakes, fish, grilled cheese, and crepes are just a few of the items that glide off this surface flawlessly. Plus, using less oil for grilling or sautéing means fewer calories.

WOODEN SPOON: This guy does pretty much everything from break up ground meat to beautifully combine the flavors in a minestrone. I personally prefer a version with a flat bottom—it stirs *and* scrapes up the deliciousness on the bottom of your pan, but without scratching your cookware.

TONGS: Imagine an extra set of hands that serve salad and pasta, snatch hot potatoes and ears of corn out of boiling water, and even flip a steak on the grill. Thanks, tongs.

BACK IN STOCK

Now let's stock that pantry.

Keep a steady supply of staples such as rice, pasta, and grains like quinoa and couscous on hand. You can create a gorgeous salad out of the nutty grain farro (high in fiber and protein) and chopped raw vegetables or even build a meal around it if you add chicken breast or salmon. I like to stockpile three types of rice—brown, jasmine, and short grain white—and a variety of pastas, like spaghetti, orecchiette (those cute little ear shapes), orzo, and bow ties.

Rather than using canned vegetables (oh, the horror . . . and high sodium!), buy fresh produce and freeze it in airtight storage bags or containers. My father taught me this trick—he freezes zucchini, corn, peas, squash, and other vegetables for up to three months. Canned tomatoes are the exception to this rule. I recommend stocking up on whole San Marzano tomatoes because they don't contain nearly as much sodium as the cubed or pureed kind.

On to seasonings. Fresh herbs like basil and mint, which typically cost about $1.99 per bunch at a grocery store, always eclipse the dried versions in flavor. (Non–spoiler alert: You can freeze herbs, too.) But certain dried spices and herbs retain their unique taste and release their essence when cooked at high temperatures. The following five seasonings are my pantry must-haves.

DRIED OREGANO: Sprinkle this piquant herb into any tomato sauce simmering on the stove for a zesty punch of flavor. Toss it with vegetables and olive oil in a plastic bag before you roast the veggies.

HERBES DE PROVENCE: Infuse roast chicken, white fish, and vegetables with a floral lightness using this French fusion of herbs like marjoram, lavender, thyme, and savory.

TURMERIC: Watch this bright, sunny yellow spice create a splash of vibrancy in any dish. Toss it with roasted sweet potatoes, cauliflower, or butternut squash. It's an anti-inflammatory too. Just be careful—it will stain everything it touches, including your hands.

FENNEL SEEDS: Gently toast and crush these sweet pods redolent of licorice and add them to turkey meatballs so they taste like they're made from pork sausage (which usually contains fennel). The crushed seeds can be life-changing in a pesto, too.

TAJÍN: You'll quickly get addicted to this peppy Mexican powder concoction of lime zest, red chili powder, and sea salt. It heightens the flavor profile of sweet fruits like mango or watermelon. I use it on everything, from chicken to popcorn to vegetables.

SHOP TILL YOU DROP

Full disclosure: Grocery shopping makes me happy. I'm that guy you see meandering through the aisles, sniffing bananas and gently squeezing baked goods. Just try tugging me away from a farmers' market. I can't help myself. But surely, you would rather have a foolproof, in-and-out twenty-minute plan for tackling your weekly jaunt to get groceries. Don't worry—I can do that, too.

First of all, have you eaten? Shopping on an empty stomach spurs poor, hasty decisions like buying a loaf of brioche bread and a jar of Nutella for dinner. (I scarfed down three of those sandwiches the night I made this mistake!) Plan to shop after eating a meal or snack.

Take stock of what's perishable in your fridge and needs to be used. Is that a ripe head of broccoli in the crisper? Make a note of it on your list so you can build a meal around it. The same goes for leftover meat and dairy items that can be repurposed in new recipes.

Now create a list of items organized by proteins, sides, and snacks. Be sure to create a list that will serve your needs for at least three days. (Or if you want bonus points from me, you can always shop day-of.) Some people cross-reference with recipes before they shop, but my tactic is to be more spontaneous: Once I select a few proteins, like ground turkey, chicken breasts, and salmon fillets, I zip to the produce section to choose complementary sides like zucchini, butternut squash, spinach, broccoli, onions, peppers, and cauliflower. Most vegetables go with any poultry, beef, pork, or fish, so don't overthink pairings. The goal is to come home laden with bags filled with fresh, nutritious food you can swiftly prepare instead of processed, ready-made meals that fill you with empty calories and regrets.

Once you're armed with a cart, follow your list like it's a treasure map. Fun fact: Most grocery stores stock their healthiest choices around the perimeter of the store. Ever notice that the dairy section seems to be a mile away from the entrance? That's intentional, and as a psychology major, I can assure you that grocery store architects and marketing masterminds know we busy humans (who are usually running a few minutes behind) dash for the closest aisles to hastily throw anything edible in our basket and get out. Don't fall victim; it's worth the few extra steps.

HIP TIP *If chicken breasts are super-cold when you cook them, they can turn out tough and rubbery. Let them rest for fifteen minutes outside of the refrigerator before you add heat.*

SALTY: Salt will bring out most ingredients' natural flavor, and it can be added to a dish to reduce bitterness. But it's not just in the flaky stuff. You'll also find it in Parmesan cheese, bacon, soy sauce, and pickled veggies. When I bake, I love to counter the sweetness of desserts by finishing with a sprinkling of salt.

BITTER: As you can imagine, bitterness should never dominate a dish. Use it to counteract an abundance of sweetness. Coffee, kale, Brussels sprouts, dark chocolate, and beer all boast a good level of bitterness.

SOUR: This taste comes from acidity—found in citrus fruits (like lemons), vinegar, green tomatoes, and yogurt—that cuts the richness of high-fat dishes served with cream sauces. Add it to temper sweetness, too. A lemon can liven up any salad, stew, or piece of meat. I love to drizzle the juice over an Italian Florentine steak; it takes the dish to a whole new level.

SWEET: Much like salty, sweet can bring out natural flavor (like when you add brown sugar to an apple pie). Add something sweet—carrots, sugar, maple syrup, honey—to a savory, salty, or sour dish to add contrast.

UMAMI: Pronounced "oooh-mommy," this taste is hard to describe if it's not in your mouth. The Japanese word for "yummy" can be found in the unique, rich, and savory taste of sundried tomatoes, miso, anchovies, and mushrooms. Add umami when a seasoned dish still feels blah, but be careful not to overdo it, as it delivers a KO punch.

WHEN YOU START COOKING AND PREPARE SOMETHING EVERY DAY, YOU REALIZE THAT YOU BECOME KNOWLEDGEABLE IN THE KITCHEN PRETTY QUICKLY. IT FEELS AMAZING TO SAY, "I CAN MAKE THAT!" AND TO FEED SOMEONE YOU LOVE.

—ANTONI

HIP TIP *With just a little kitchen wisdom and a few flavorful ingredients, you can create a meal that nourishes both the body and the soul.*

GENIUS KITCHEN HACKS

Can I tell you how many avocado questions I have gotten since I showed everyone how to efficiently remove a pit on Queer Eye? Clearly, you all love a culinary shortcut, so herewith, some more of my favorite hacks:

Dry spices like cumin and fennel become even more pungent and aromatic if you toast them for a few minutes before you add them to a dish. The same goes for raw nuts. Just watch closely because both burn fast.

To give butter a more nuanced, nutty flavor, whisk it over medium heat for two to three minutes, until it browns slightly. Then substitute it for regular melted butter in recipes or lightly drizzle on veggies.

Got a bottle of wine that you can't finish but don't want to waste? Pour the vino into an ice cube tray and use those cubes for cooking sauces or making a more potent sangria. Do the same with leftover coffee or espresso to make caffeine cubes for iced lattes.

Add leftover fresh herbs like rosemary to a bottle of olive oil to infuse it with flavor.

PAGING INSPIRATION

Cookbooks have always had a huge influence on me. When I was a kid, my parents would return from trips to foreign countries with a big batch of them. (It adds so much weight to your luggage, though . . . Who does that?) One time, they came home from Marrakesh with cookbooks and smoked fish wrapped in a carpet. That didn't end well.

There are three cookbooks I constantly reference for inspiration, guidance, and a good laugh:

Feast **by Nigella Lawson.** There's such sensuality to her writing and a deep respect for food. I love that she's not a chef, per se, but passionately cooks for her family and loved ones.

Mastering the Art of French Cooking **by Julia Child, Simone Beck, and Louisette Bertholle.** The fact that Julia Child re-created French recipes for Americans and that this book came out when she was forty-nine is amazing. It's never too late to start doing what you love.

In My Kitchen: 100 Recipes and Discoveries for Passionate Cooks **by Ted Allen.** I learned so much from my mentor dear Ted Allen that it makes me happy to flip through his book and try his recipes. The book delivers a handy mishmash of great recipes for everything from deviled eggs to pork buns—with lots of sumptuous pictures of food and his huge kitchen in Brooklyn, where I cooked for him.

HIP TIP *Instead of baking or sautéing veggies, for infinite flavor crank up the oven to 450°F and roast them on a pan lined with parchment paper.*

START THE CLOCK

Most of us get stymied by preparing the main course, aka the protein of our meal. Here are three suggestions for proteins that you can cook easily and efficiently, according to your schedule.

10 MINUTES

Gently whisk 3 eggs in a bowl until the yolk and whites are blended. Throw a pat of butter into a nonstick pan on medium-high, then pour the eggs into the pan and let them bubble until the liquid solidifies. Now add any leftover veggies, like cooked spinach or broccoli or potatoes, and add slices of a creamy cheese like Havarti or goat to bind your ingredients (sour cream works, too). Fold over browned sides to create a rustic country omelet for two.

15 MINUTES

Put a tablespoon of apple cider vinegar, a teaspoon of grainy mustard, and a ¼ cup of heavy cream in a cast iron skillet over medium heat and stir into a rich sauce. Throw two pork chops into the pan and cook for 6 minutes on each side. Dinner is served.

20 MINUTES

Pound a chicken breast to a ½-inch thickness (with a kitchen mallet or even a hammer covered in plastic wrap). Dip it into a beaten egg and then drag the cutlet in panko or breadcrumbs mixed with a tablespoon or two of grated Parmesan cheese, pressing to make sure it sticks. Add one inch of peanut or vegetable oil to a nonstick pan and cook chicken for 4 to 5 minutes on each side. Yum.

TOO MANY MANY QUEERS IN THE KITCHEN

After a long day of shooting Queer Eye, someone inevitably shrieks, "I'm starving! What should we eat?"—and everyone looks at me. But the truth is, we all have food personalities. If Karamo had his way, we would subsist on Skittles, even though he has a cache of amazing Jamaican recipes from his grandmother; Jonathan loves anything smothered in melted cheese; Tan has a sweet tooth and could literally outbake us all; while Bobby is on a vegan kick and will wash anything down with a margarita.

I asked the guys to share their signature dishes. Guess what? You can tell a lot about a man by his go-to recipe.

ANTONI'S LAZY BOLOGNESE SAUCE

SERVES 6

Typically, I'll make a pot of whole-wheat spaghetti and whip up this turkey Bolognese in 20 minutes when the boys get hangry. I like to reverse the ratio of pasta to sauce, so there's basically a dish of sauce with some pasta floating in it. That way, you get protein and veggies, but you don't end up in a carb coma. You could even try zucchini noodles.

¼ cup extra-virgin olive oil

1 yellow onion, chopped

4 garlic cloves, minced

½ cup fresh peas

1 pound ground turkey (dark meat)

3 cups canned whole San Marzano tomatoes

¼ cup toasted pine nuts

Kosher salt and freshly ground black pepper

Cooked pasta of your choice, to serve

Freshly grated Parmesan, to finish

1. Heat the oil in a heavy large frying pan over medium heat. Add the onion and garlic and sauté until the onions are soft and translucent, about 5 minutes. Throw in the peas and let them cook for 2 minutes.

2. Add the ground turkey and cook, breaking it up with a wooden spoon, until it's mostly no longer pink, about 3 minutes.

3. Add the whole tomatoes, reduce the heat to medium-low, and simmer gently, stirring often, for 15 minutes, to allow the flavors to blend. Stir in the toasted pine nuts. Season the sauce to taste.

4. Add the sauce to the pasta of your choice. Top with freshly grated Parmesan to finish.

5. The sauce can be made ahead. Let the sauce cool completely before transferring it to a container with a lid and refrigerating it for up to a week, or freezing it for up to three months.

KARAMO'S JERK CHICKEN WINGS

SERVES 4 TO 6

I love finding fun ways to merge both my cultures, and this recipe doesn't keep me stuck in the kitchen. It was handed down from my Jamaican grandmother.

Cooking spray

3 pounds chicken wing drumettes

5 tablespoons yellow scotch bonnet pepper sauce
  or habanero sauce (adjust to your liking)

2 teaspoons seasoned salt (I like Lawry's)

2 teaspoons ground onions

½ teaspoon ground cumin

2 teaspoons dried garlic

2 teaspoons ground black pepper

3 tablespoons brown sugar

2 teaspoons vegetable oil

1. Preheat the oven to 450°F. Line a baking sheet with aluminum foil and spray with cooking spray.

2. Place the chicken in a large bowl and rinse under warm water for 2 minutes. Drain and pat the bowl dry.

3. Combine the pepper sauce, seasoned salt, ground onions, ground cumin, dried garlic, ground black pepper, brown sugar, and vegetable oil in the same bowl. Add the chicken, turn to coat, and massage the marinade into the meat for about 3 minutes. Make sure each piece is evenly covered. Let it sit for 5 minutes to allow the flavors to be absorbed.

4. Arrange the chicken drumettes on the prepared baking sheet and bake for 25 minutes. An instant-read thermometer inserted near the bone should read 165°F to ensure the meat is cooked through.

5. Remove chicken drumettes from the oven and let rest on the baking sheet for 5 minutes before transferring to a platter. Serve.

TAN'S CARROT CAKE

MAKES TWO 9-INCH ROUND LAYERS OR ONE 9 X 13-INCH SHEET CAKE

I find it calming to bake because I like doing something with my hands. I don't think it's that dissimilar to what I used to do in fashion. To go from a pattern to an end garment, there's math involved, and you have to precisely follow steps.

For the cake

2 cups granulated sugar

2¼ cups all-purpose flour

1 teaspoon baking powder

1 teaspoon kosher salt

1 teaspoon baking soda

1 teaspoon cinnamon

1 cup vegetable oil

4 eggs

3 cups grated carrot

For the frosting

2 cups powdered sugar

½ cup butter, softened

1 (3-ounce) package cream cheese, softened

1 teaspoon vanilla extract

¼ teaspoon ground nutmeg

1. Make the cake. Preheat the oven to 375°F.

2. In a large bowl, stir together the sugar, flour, baking powder, salt, baking soda, and cinnamon. Add the oil and eggs and stir to combine. Fold in the carrot to mix evenly.

3. Transfer the batter to two greased 9-inch round cake pans or a greased 9 x 13-inch baking dish and bake for 30 to 35 minutes, until a tester inserted in the center comes out clean.

4. Meanwhile, make the frosting. Using an electric mixer, in a separate large bowl, beat together the powdered sugar, butter, cream cheese, vanilla, and nutmeg until whipped.

5. Let the cake cool completely before frosting. (If you're making a round layer cake, frost between the layers as well as on top; leave the sides naked.) Slice and serve.

BOBBY'S ORANGE MINT TEQUILA MAGIC

MAKES ONE DRINK

I suppose you could consider me the Fab Five's resident mixolo-gist. A cocktail on the roof at sunset is the best way to unwind and shrug off the day. This light, refreshing tequila drink has a burst of mint flavor that surprises you.

¼ orange, halved and peel removed

6-7 fresh mint leaves

1½ ounces Cointreau

2½ ounces silver or blanco tequila

Ice

Club soda

1. Place the orange pieces, mint, and Cointreau into a highball glass. Using a muddler or the end of a wooden spoon, muddle the ingredients together until the orange releases its juice and the mint releases its oils.

2. Add the tequila, fill the glass with ice, and add as much club soda as you like. Stir to combine. Cheers!

JONATHAN'S HAMBURGER CASSEROLE

SERVES 4

I don't do recipes, really, which is why I don't cook that well. I take more of a "freehand" approach. I got the idea for this casserole by watching Rachael Ray make a layered ice cream cake about twenty years ago. Yumm-o!

1. So, you take four potatoes and you boil them. Then you mash them with the skin on and add diced garlic, some sour cream, some milk, and some butter. You just eyeball how much you want in there and make it into mashed potatoes. (I'm sure Antoni would frown upon that. Whatever.)

2. Then, you take that potato mixture and put it into the bottom of an oval baking dish. Now add a pound of ground hamburger meat that you browned earlier on the stove with some chopped onions and green peppers or any other veggies you have around. (You can use ground turkey or fake meat if you want.) Layer that on top of the mashed potatoes.

3. Then, finally, sprinkle on a blanket of fun cheese like provolone or pepper jack. If you're feeling fancy, take string cheese and make like a pie and lattice it. (I know, right?)

4. Bake that girl at 350ºF for about 20 minutes, till the cheese is bubbly and broily. Four lucky people get to share this dish. Um, you're all welcome!

WHAT'LL YOU HAVE?

Dining out is the best way to expand your taste vocabulary and pick up new tips you can use at home. When you think about it, going to a restaurant for dinner is almost like traveling. You leave your home kitchen behind to explore other regional cuisines and experience new flavor profiles. That's one way to rationalize eating out twice in a week: You're not too lazy to cook or go grocery shopping—wink, wink—you're broadening your culinary horizons and doing research.

With that in mind, try to avoid ordering anything at a restaurant that's easy to prepare at home. That lineup includes burgers, chicken breasts, salmon, and pasta. Why not try a dish that you wouldn't tackle on a weeknight, like pulled pork or short ribs? (Both take hours to do the right way.) Choosing meals off the menu that call for more expertise, or that you have never tried or even heard of, is a great way to sample a dish and learn.

I get that menus can be intimidating, especially when you consider the foreign words and fancy food terms you may encounter. I recently saw a study that claimed 59 percent of people who recently ate out had been afraid to order a dish because they didn't recognize an ingredient. That's a shame. As a former waiter, I'm here to tell you that your server is your ally. (It's likely that when he started working at the restaurant, he didn't know his crudo from his confit, either.) When I don't recognize a cut of meat or a cooking term or an ingredient, I simply say, "I'm not familiar with this word. Can you please describe it to me?" Asking a server to describe it means you will also get a sense of its taste and texture. Don't be shy about asking for recommendations either. There's no better compliment to a server than to be asked for his or her favorite dish. "But what do you love?" I always inquire with a smile. That bit of trust establishes a bond between you and your server—and he or she will go the extra mile to make your meal spectacular.

ANOTHER REASON TO EAT OUT

Looking for dinner party inspo? Hit a beloved restaurant and take note of every detail. Listen to the soundtrack, assess the lighting, and check out the art. You can even mentally measure the time between courses to get a sense of the cadence of a superb meal. There's a reason they call it a dining room. All the elements of entertaining are in play right in front of you.

HIP TIP *After cooking beef, let it rest for ten minutes per pound to allow juices to settle and be absorbed. Otherwise, the juices will run out and the meat will taste dry.*

Feeding someone else is a service. It's the ultimate act of love and care you can pass on to another person.

—ANTONI

ON THE VINE

*Anyone who's worked in a restaurant will tell you with cer-*tainty that the wine list causes more panic for diners than an inflated bill. Especially when someone on a first date or at a business dinner is in charge of ordering for the table. My advice is to first do a little homework. Lots of restaurants have online menus and wine lists. If that's not the case and you're incredibly anxious, pop by the eatery before your reservation and ask for a copy of the wine list. Simply let them know that you want to do some reconnaissance and promise to discreetly return it when you arrive for your meal. Then, turn to the Internet for tasting notes.

Ultimately though, you're overlooking an expert if you don't consult with your sommelier or server. That person should know every wine's notes firsthand. Tasting, too, is the most visceral way to get educated. Here's a little secret that no sommelier will tell you: Because most people order the second cheapest wine on the list, that bottle is marked up the most. (Or it's a subpar wine that they want to unload.) Instead, go for the most reasonable option if you're on a budget, because it's probably a better bottle. Put the savings toward an order of crème brûlée.

But you don't need to be a wine aficionado out of the gate. Honing an appreciation for this subtle intoxicant, much like learning to cook, is an ongoing education. Trust me, even your haughty coworker who brags about his cellar of vintage Bordeaux doesn't know every single varietal. And unless you envision yourself with a second career as a sommelier, you don't need to familiarize yourself with every vintage and vine, either.

I always tell friends that the best way to learn about wines is to taste as many as you can—and start with one region. If you find that you're a fan of big, heady reds, focus on Malbecs out of Chile or Argentina. Prefer a subtler, fruit-forward sip? California Pinot Noirs and French Beaujolais fit the bill. White wines, too, share characteristics by origin. Look to an Italian Pinot Grigio for a dry, crisp taste with mild acidity on the tongue. A Gewürztraminer from the Alsace region of Germany tickles your palate with aromas of peaches and rose petals.

Intrigued? Further educate yourself online, visit a local vineyard, browse a wine shop, and ask lots of questions. Most important, find a varietal that you like, whether it's an oaky Chardonnay that's as friendly as a puppy or a bold, complex Cabernet Sauvignon that leaves you scratching your head but wanting another sip. Then, explore that particular wine fully and then find another varietal that's like it. Look: Now you're a pseudo-expert in two wines.

"Some people think cooking is about rules; I'm not one of them."

SHAKEN OR STIRRED?

You don't need to muddle mint like a mixologist to make guests happy in your home. Start small with a manageable bar that covers the essentials. No one will smirk at a silky smooth martini or turn their nose up at an aromatic gin and tonic. Both of those cocktails are comprised of just two basic ingredients (minus a garnish), so embrace their simplicity.

And where do you begin when it comes to stocking up? Pick up these spirits and mixers that are most requested. Just be sure to store liquor in a cool place away from direct sunlight; vermouth, for martinis, should be refrigerated after opening because it's technically a wine.

When it comes to tools, a bartender doesn't need more than five utensils to get down to business.

VODKA **SINGLE MALT SCOTCH** **VERMOUTH**

TEQUILA **TONIC WATER**

GIN **CLUB SODA**

For both bar aesthetics and to add piquancy to cocktails, I like to display a few beautiful bottles like Campari (a fiery red bittersweet liqueur), Cointreau (an orange liqueur), or St. Germain (a light, fragrant liqueur made from elderflower essence).

BAR SPOON **MUDDLER** **JIGGER** **COCKTAIL SHAKER** **STRAINER**

And don't get anxious about glassware. You only need four to six of the basic styles: a short glass, a tall glass, and stemware for wine. Bobby loves stemless wineglasses because they're modern, more durable, and can serve as cocktail glasses in a pinch. You can get some martini glasses if that's your style, too.

When it comes to ice cubes, invest in a tray that makes jumbo-sized chunks, because they last longer, don't water down your drink, and look pretty damn cool.

BOBBY LOVES A BAR CART

Ah, the beloved booze wagon. Never mind its utilitarian abilities as a bar back, this portable cabinet also doubles as a general declutterer. Bobby loves to roll one into a kitchen and store organized utensils, small appliances, and even neatly arranged spices on its shelves. He calls it "instant counter space." Love that!

HIP TIP *Make your own cold brew coffee by steeping ground coffee beans in water overnight in a French press you put in the fridge.*

Five-Minute Make-Better: Fruit Stays Fresh

A drizzle of lemon juice will keep apple slices from browning for an hour or so, but a combo of one part honey to two parts water prevents discoloring of apples, pears, peaches, and other sliced stone fruits for up to eight hours. The peptides in honey halt the oxidation process. To preserve fruit salad for a party the next day or prep a bar with fruits for garnish, soak the slices in a bowl of the honey/water mixture for one minute to ensure a day's worth of freshness.

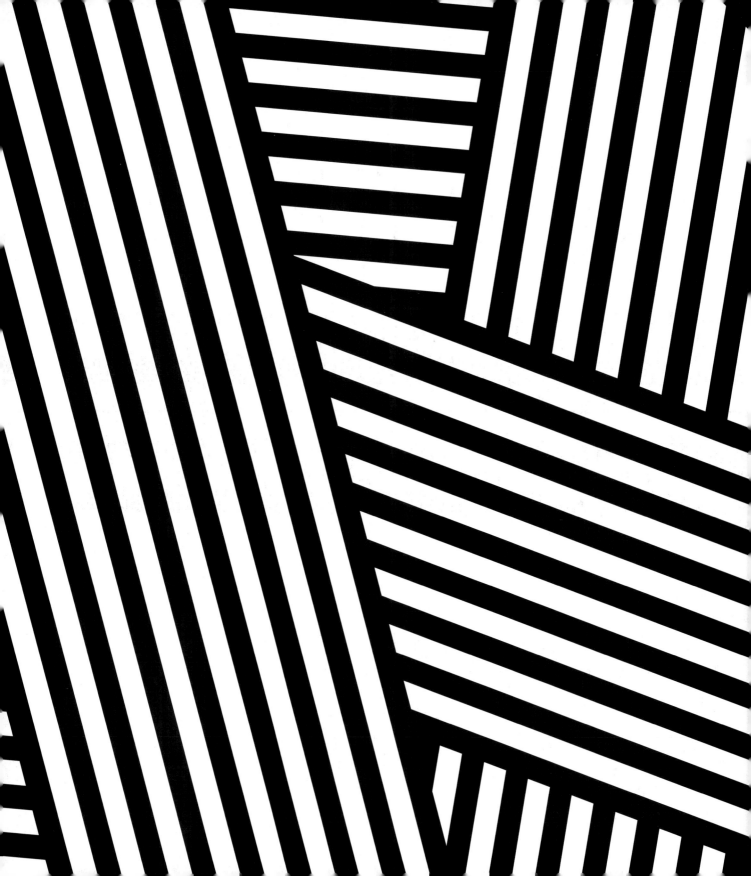

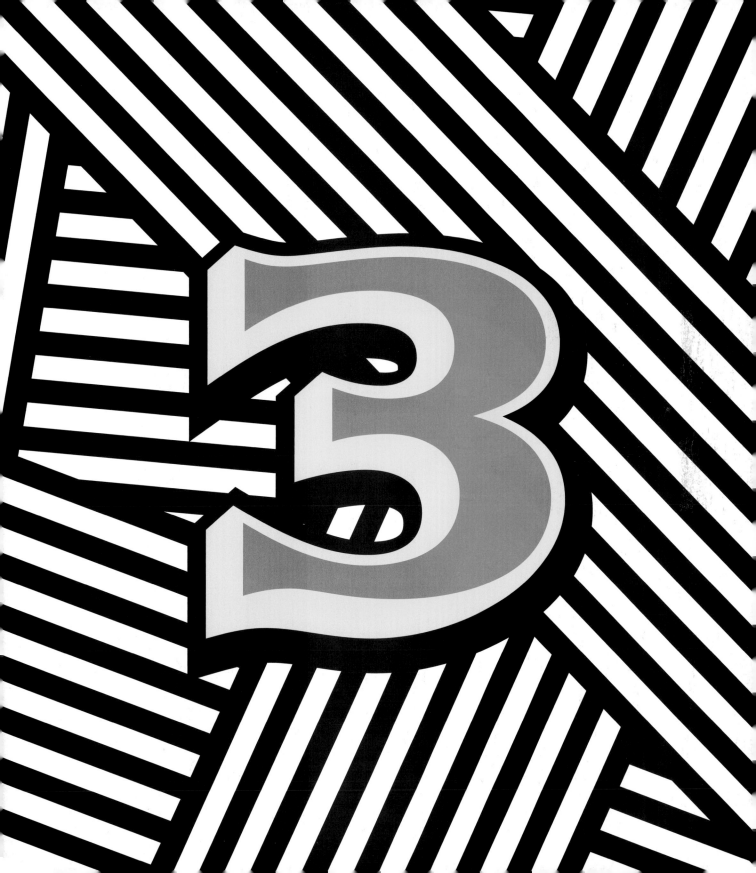

COME TOGETHER

Can you believe—it's almost time to go! Trust us, we might cry, too. But what better way to say goodbye and thank you so much for joining us on this journey than to have you over for a decadent, debaucherous dinner party? Remember all those tips we passed along earlier? Well, we're about to come together and put some of them to use as we show you how to set a stand-out table, select killer music, create an amazing menu, dress to thrill, and connect with your guests on a decidedly deeper level. You don't need to bring anything except your best self.

GRACE, GRATITUDE, AND GOALS WITH KARAMO

My version of saying grace before a meal doesn't stop at being thankful for the delicious food on our plates. That's a given, and I always call out whoever cooked over a hot stove—or ordered in, if that's the case—for their loving contributions. Afterward, I like to invite everyone at the table to take a turn talking about personal gratitude. This is the moment where we acknowledge the aspects of our lives we appreciate the most. I always start and let everyone know that the table is a safe zone to speak from the heart.

Once we're all eating, there are a few deep questions I like to throw out to the group to provoke fiery dialogue.

- *You have twenty-four hours to live. What are you going to do?*
- *Tonight, you're a superhero. What's your superpower—and why?*
- *Tell us your definition of "joy" right now.*
- *Whom do you love and how are you showing it?*
- *What's your personal make-better?*

Finally, over dessert, I like to hit on what we all want to achieve in the next year. So I ask everyone at the table to take turns in talking about a personal goal. This is a great opportunity for everyone else to weigh in with helpful suggestions and support.

BOBBY LAYS OUT THE TABLESCAPE

Think of your dining room table as a blank canvas. If you were to paint that stretch of white, would you add vibrant color or stick with a more monochromatic palette? Like the menu and the music, your tablescape is entirely subjective and should always reflect you and the tone you want to set for your meal.

START WITH YOUR FLOWERS. That's my approach to a tablescape, because the flowers are usually the focal point of the spread. Avoid heavily scented blooms that overpower the room and oversized centerpieces that make it hard for guests to see each other. I love a graceful, elegant orchid because it lasts for months and will continue to remind you of the evening.

LINENS MAKE A DIFFERENCE. You don't have to splurge on an expensive tablecloth and napkins—the effect can still be elegant. For someone like Tan, who loves his black jeans, I opt for dark linens that won't leave a film of white lint on the laps of my guests.

LAYER THOSE PLATES. If you're serving a few courses, be sure to stack your salad or soup dishes atop dinner plates so it's easier to serve or clear the table. I'm a proponent of inexpensive all-white that can easily be replaced or hide chips in case things get rowdy. Stemless wineglasses can double as cocktail glasses. (Also, Jonathan has a bad habit of elbowing wineglasses when he is gesticulating, so we avoid those when possible.)

WELCOME GUESTS TO THEIR SEATS. Regular place cards do the trick, but this is an opportunity to get creative. I love the look of displaying copies of photos in small 2¾ x 3¾ frames that guests can take home with them after an event, or even scattering different-sized framed photos along a long table, like a runner of memories.

MAKE IT SEXY. Nobody looks good in overhead lighting—not even Antoni! Dim, diffused lighting and scattered candles—always unscented on a dining table—create a romantic and flattering setting.

JONATHAN'S SUPPERTIME SOUNDTRACK

Nobody knows better than me how music sets the mood. A dinner party playlist has to serve up love, authenticity, positivity, and maybe even a little pain. That's how we all heal. Pass the Champagne, please.

COCKTAIL HOUR
Solange, *A Seat at the Table*

It's one of my favorite albums PERIOD. The subject matter is deep, so just listening to the lyrics will definitely start some great conversations. On top of the music are gorgeous background vocals that give me life! It's a true masterpiece, and I've said it before, she's a style icon. We can talk about her clothes over cocktails, for sure.

APPETIZERS
SZA, *CTRL*

I just can't stop with this album. I annoyed my boys with this one because, again, I can't stop. I'm spinning these songs during appetizers because I am so hungry for her music, and once I get a taste, I devour it. I'm sure you will, too.

MAIN COURSE
Hamilton: An American Musical

You can't tell me that this isn't amazing dinner party music. This musical is a *feast*. So many different genres, and you're being educated the whole time. We're feeding our stomachs, our souls, and our minds.

DESSERT
Dua Lipa, Dua Lipa

Everyone knows Dua Lipa is my girl, so I have to include this beautiful, soulful album because it's a sweet treat. I love her voice, like her actual voice. But I also love how she writes. I get her. I'm here for it.

LAST CALL
Ariana Grande, *Dangerous Woman*

Let's be real. If we're still having cocktails at this point, the night is probably just getting started. I love this album because she's giving us pop realness and beautiful ballads. Oh, and who's joining us on a song? It's one of my other faves, Nicki Minaj. This is the soundtrack for a good time!

DROP THE MIC

Which songs get us onstage and vamping like Vegas divas? These are our usual karaoke requests. Turn them on and watch your party turn up.

Jonathan: "Bleeding Love" by Leona Lewis. It has ups, it has downs, and it's also perfect for a gentle wind in the hair.

Tan: "Someone Like You" by Adele. This song takes me back to that feeling of being dumped—and it gets me every time.

Antoni: "Hero" by Enrique Iglesias. I excel at all his songs, but "Hero" is a little less falsetto-y, so it's my strongest.

Karamo: "Can't Nobody Hold Me Down" by Puff Daddy and Mase. It's such a bad boy song and I definitely have fun with it.

Bobby: I hate singing, but I'm happy to judge your performances.

A dinner party falls flat when you only check the boxes. Make sure to put your own stamp on it.

THE MENU

~~

Appetizers

•

Marinated Goat Cheese

Spinach Pie

Entrées

•

Mustard-Crusted Salmon
with White Beans and
Spinach

Beef Tenderloin with Thyme
and Red Wine Sauce

Prosciutto-Wrapped
Chicken with Fontina and
Arugula Salad

Roasted Sausages and Grapes

Bucatini with Asparagus
and Peas

Vegetables

•

Fresh Corn *off* the Cob

Roasted Butternut Squash
with Tahini Sauce

Desserts

•

The Absolute Best
Chocolate Cookies

Easy Almond Cake with
Fresh Fruit

NOW LET'S EAT

We wanted to share some of our favorite party recipes with you—the ones we've made over and over again for dinner parties, potlucks, holiday meals, barbecues, and just fun nights with friends. Feel free to use these to design your own menu, supplementing with your own recipes however you like. Just make sure we have a seat at the table, k?

MARINATED GOAT CHEESE
Serves 8

This easy-to-make appetizer is always a hit and seems *much* fancier than it is. Work it, honey!

   1 (11- to 12-ounce) log of goat cheese

   1 cup extra-virgin olive oil

   3 to 4 bay leaves

   1 tablespoon mixed peppercorns (black, white, green)

   3 sprigs of fresh thyme (or 1 tablespoon dried)

   4 garlic cloves, thinly sliced

   ½ cup thinly sliced basil

   1 tablespoon pink peppercorns

   Crackers or French baguette, to serve

Slice the goat cheese into ½-inch rounds. Arrange in a shallow 9 x 13-inch baking dish.

Heat the olive oil, bay leaves, mixed peppercorns, and thyme in a small saucepan over medium-high heat until the oil begins to sizzle. Remove the pan from the stove and pour the mixture over the goat cheese.

Sprinkle the garlic over the cheese and add the basil and pink peppercorns. Serve with your favorite crackers or a sliced baguette alongside.

SPINACH PIE
Serves 8

This "spanakopita" (Greek for "spinach pie") recipe is one of our favorites: crispy phyllo filled with a delicious mixture of spinach, feta cheese, and dill.

   4 tablespoons (½ stick) unsalted butter, plus ¾ cup (1½ sticks) melted butter

   ½ cup minced onion

   3 (10-ounce) packages frozen chopped spinach, thawed and water squeezed out

   3 medium eggs

   ½ pound feta cheese, crumbled

   ¼ cup chopped flat-leaf parsley

   2 tablespoons chopped fresh dill

   1 teaspoon kosher salt

   Freshly ground pepper, to taste

   1 (1-pound) box frozen phyllo dough

Preheat the oven to 350°F.

Melt 4 tablespoons butter in a skillet over medium heat. Add the onion and sauté until it's beginning to turn golden, about 5 minutes. Add the spinach and cook, stirring, just to warm through, about 2 minutes. Remove the pan from the heat.

Beat the eggs in a large bowl. Stir in the feta, parsley, dill, salt, and pepper. Add the spinach mixture and stir well to combine.

Brush the bottom of a 9 x 13-inch baking dish with the melted butter. Layer in 8 sheets of phyllo, brushing each with butter, so the bottom of the dish is completely covered. Spread half of the spinach mixture over the dough, leaving a ½-inch border all around. Add 8 more sheets of phyllo dough, again brushing each with butter. Repeat with the rest of the spinach mixture and 8 more phyllo sheets to create another layer. Brush the remaining melted butter over the top layer.

Using a very sharp knife, score the top layer of dough, creating 2- to 3-inch slices all around. Bake for 30 to 35 minutes, until golden.

Let the spinach pie cool for 5 minutes, then slice and serve.

MUSTARD-CRUSTED SALMON WITH WHITE BEANS AND SPINACH

Serves 8

This salmon recipe is sure to become your new go-to. Based on a French bistro classic, it really doesn't get any tastier than this.

For the salmon

> 8 pieces of skinless salmon fillet
>   (8 to 10 ounces each)
>
> 2 teaspoons kosher salt or sea salt
>
> Freshly ground pepper
>
> ¼ cup Dijon mustard
>
> 8 tablespoons panko bread crumbs
>
> 2 to 3 tablespoons canola oil

For the beans and spinach

> 6 tablespoons extra-virgin olive oil
>
> 2 pounds fresh baby spinach

> 2 (15-ounce) cans white beans, drained and
>   rinsed
>
> Kosher salt and freshly ground pepper

Preheat the oven to 500°F.

Season the salmon on both sides with salt and pepper. On the rounded side of each piece, spread about 2 teaspoons of mustard, then sprinkle on 1 tablespoon panko, pressing it into the mustard.

Heat the oil in a large ovenproof sauté pan over high heat. When the oil is shimmering, carefully add the salmon coated-side down. Reduce the heat to medium and sear until the mustard and bread crumbs form a crust, about 2 minutes. Flip the salmon using a spatula and sear the other side for 1 minute more.

Transfer the sauté pan to the oven and cook for 3 or 4 minutes more, until firm.

Meanwhile, make the spinach. Heat 3 tablespoons olive oil in a large nonstick skillet over medium heat. Add the spinach one handful at a time and cook until wilted down, 1 to 2 minutes per addition. Drain off any liquid from the pan. Add the beans and the remaining olive oil and cook until warmed through, 1 to 2 minutes. Season with salt and pepper.

Divide the spinach and bean mixture among plates, place the mustard-crusted salmon on top, and serve.

BEEF TENDERLOIN WITH THYME AND RED WINE SAUCE

Serves 8

For the red-meat lovers in your life, nothing beats this classic roasted beef tenderloin with a deeply flavored red wine sauce.

For the beef

1 beef tenderloin (5 to 6 pounds), trimmed

Kosher salt and freshly ground pepper

30 thyme sprigs

Extra-virgin olive oil

For the red wine sauce

5 tablespoons (⅓ cup) unsalted butter

5 shallots, thinly sliced

2 cups dry red wine (we like Cabernet, Pinot Noir, or Merlot)

2 tablespoons balsamic or red wine vinegar

6 rosemary sprigs

4 cups beef broth

Kosher salt and freshly ground pepper

Preheat the oven to 250°F.

Make the beef. Season the beef with salt and pepper. Fold the narrow piece of the tenderloin under and tie at 1-inch intervals with kitchen twine. Tuck the thyme sprigs under the twine all around the beef. Brush all over with olive oil and place beef in a roasting pan.

Roast for about 2 hours, until an instant-read thermometer inserted in the thickest part reads 130°F for medium rare.

Meanwhile, when the beef is about half-way done cooking, make the sauce. Melt 2 tablespoons butter in large sauté pan over medium-low heat. Add the shallots and sauté until soft and translucent, about 10 minutes.

Increase the heat to high and add the wine and vinegar, scraping up any browned bits from the bottom of the pan with a wooden spoon. Cook for about 10 minutes, until liquid has reduced to a thick syrup. Add the rosemary sprigs and beef broth and cook for another 20 minutes, until reduced to about 1 cup.

Pour the mixture through a fine-mesh strainer set over a medium bowl. Just before serving, whisk the remaining butter into the sauce. Season with salt and pepper to taste.

Transfer the roasted beef to a cutting board, cover with foil, and let rest for about 20 minutes. Carve into ½-inch slices and serve with red wine sauce alongside.

PROSCIUTTO-WRAPPED CHICKEN WITH FONTINA AND ARUGULA SALAD
Serves 8

This is a quick and easy take on traditional Italian chicken saltimbocca. Tons of flavor for very little effort. The arugula side salad adds a refreshing brightness to the rich and salty dish—and it goes with pretty much anything.

8 boneless, skinless chicken breasts (8 to 10 ounces each)

8 ounces Fontina (or other soft Italian cheese), cut into 8 pieces

3 tablespoons fresh tarragon leaves

16 slices prosciutto

2 tablespoons extra-virgin olive oil, plus more for the salad

8 to 10 ounces arugula

1 lemon

Preheat the oven to 350°F.

Cut a 2-inch pocket along the thick side of each chicken breast, taking care not to cut through to the other side. Stuff a piece of cheese into each pocket. Season the outside of the chicken breasts with salt and pepper and sprinkle with tarragon.

Wrap 2 pieces of prosciutto around each chicken breast. If necessary, secure with toothpicks.

Heat the oil in large sauté pan over medium-high heat. When the oil is shimmering, working in batches, sear the chicken breasts, about 4 to 5 minutes per side, flipping halfway through, until no longer pink on the outside. Add more oil as needed. Transfer the seared chicken breasts to a baking sheet.

Bake the chicken breasts for about 10 minutes, until an instant-read thermometer inserted in the thickest part of one reads 165°F. Remove the chicken from the oven and let rest for 5 minutes.

Meanwhile, in a large bowl, add the arugula. Squeeze the lemon over the greens, drizzle with olive oil, and season with salt and pepper. Toss to combine.

Serve family style with the arugula salad alongside the chicken on a platter.

ROASTED SAUSAGES AND GRAPES
Serves 8

Sausage and grapes are a classic Italian pairing. We recommend serving this one with mashed potatoes or polenta.

1½ pounds sweet Italian sausage

1½ pounds hot Italian sausage

4 tablespoons (½ stick) unsalted butter

5 cups mixed red and green seedless grapes (about 2 pounds)

¼ cup dry red wine (we like Cabernet, Pinot Noir, or Merlot)

4 tablespoons balsamic vinegar

Preheat the oven to 450°F.

Bring a large pot of water to a boil over high heat. Prick the sausages all over using a fork. Add the sausages to the boiling water and parboil to release some of the fat, 5 to 7 minutes, then drain.

Melt the butter in a large roasting pan over medium-high heat. Add the grapes and toss to coat. Add the wine and stir until reduced by half, 10 to 15 minutes. Add the sausages and stir to mix evenly with the grapes.

Transfer the pan to the oven and roast for 20 to 25 minutes, until the sausages are browned, turning them once after 10 minutes.

Return the pan to the stove over medium-high heat. Add the balsamic vinegar and cook until the liquid is syrupy, 5 to 10 minutes, stirring the liquid occasionally and scraping up any browned bits from the bottom.

Transfer the sausages, grapes, and sauce to a platter and serve.

BUCATINI WITH ASPARAGUS AND PEAS
Serves 8

This recipe takes the classic *cacio e pepe* (cheese and pepper) pasta and celebrates spring's specialties with the addition of fresh asparagus and peas.

Sea salt

1 pound bucatini, spaghetti, or linguini

1 pound thin asparagus

½ pound sugar snap peas, trimmed

1 cup fresh or frozen peas

4 tablespoons (½ stick) salted butter

1 tablespoon freshly ground pepper

¾ cup grated Pecorino Romano cheese, plus more to finish

¾ cup grated Parmesan cheese, plus more to finish

Extra-virgin olive oil, to finish

Bring a large pot of water to a boil over high heat and add 2 tablespoons salt. Add the pasta and cook until not quite al dente (a couple minutes less than suggested on the package instructions). Add the asparagus, snap peas, and peas. Cook for 1 minute until the vegetables are bright green. Reserve 1 cup of pasta cooking water and drain all the ingredients.

Melt 2 tablespoons butter in a large sauté pan over medium heat. Add the pepper and sauté for 1 minute, then add ½ cup of the reserved pasta cooking water and the remaining 2 tablespoons butter. Stir vigorously until the mixture is thickened, about 1 minute.

Add the cooked pasta and vegetables and the grated cheeses to the pan. Toss until the cheese is melted and the pasta is al dente, about 1 minute. Add more pasta cooking water if needed to adjust the texture of the sauce to your liking.

Season with more salt, sprinkle with more cheese, and drizzle with olive oil before serving.

FRESH CORN *OFF* THE COB

Serves 8

Corn is probably our favorite summer veg. This fresh, creamy, herby take is the perfect complement to any main course. Dine al fresco tonight!

8 ears of corn, shucked and cleaned

6 tablespoons (¾ stick) salted butter

1 small yellow onion, diced

Kosher salt and freshly ground pepper

¼ cup fresh herbs of your choice (we like sage, rosemary, thyme, and chives)

Slice the corn kernels straight off the cob with a sharp knife.

Melt 4 tablespoons butter in large pan over medium-low heat. Add the onion and a pinch of salt and cook for 5 to 6 minutes, stirring occasionally, until soft and translucent. Add the corn and 3 tablespoons water and cook until the corn is tender, 2 to 3 minutes more.

Transfer half the sautéed corn to a food processor and puree until smooth. Return the pureed corn to the pan and stir in the remaining butter. Stir in the fresh herbs and season with salt and pepper. Serve warm.

ROASTED BUTTERNUT SQUASH WITH TAHINI SAUCE

Serves 8

This dish boasts rich, roasted squash and chickpeas with a delicious sesame dressing. It's full of flavor. Enjoy it alongside any autumn meal, or even on its own as a salad.

4 tablespoons extra-virgin olive oil

1½ tablespoons curry powder

¼ teaspoon cayenne pepper

3 cups cubed butternut squash

2 (15-ounce) cans chickpeas, drained and rinsed

Kosher salt

2 (8- to 10-ounce) bags baby spinach or
 baby kale

¾ cup chopped flat-leaf parsley or cilantro

For the tahini sauce

4 tablespoons tahini

½ cup extra-virgin olive oil

2 tablespoons white wine vinegar

2 teaspoons honey or brown sugar

1 teaspoon kosher salt

Preheat the oven to 425°F. Line a baking
sheet with foil.

In a large bowl, combine the olive oil, curry
powder, and cayenne pepper. Let sit for 10
minutes to allow the flavors to meld. Add
the squash and chickpeas and stir to coat
completely. Transfer to the prepared pan,
spacing apart, and season with salt. Roast
until the squash is tender and the chickpeas
are crispy, 15 to 20 minutes.

Meanwhile, make the tahini sauce. Combine
the tahini, olive oil, vinegar, honey, and salt
in a glass jar and shake to mix thoroughly.

In a large bowl, combine the spinach,
parsley, roasted squash, and chickpeas. Pour
the tahini sauce on top and toss to combine.
Before serving, let the salad sit for about
15 minutes, until the greens are wilted and
the flavors meld.

THE ABSOLUTE BEST CHOCOLATE COOKIES

Makes 12 to 18 cookies

Need we say more? The fleur de sel is
the secret, delicious accent to these
crumbly chocolate cookies. Sweet *and*
salty . . . mmm.

2½ cups all-purpose flour

¾ cup cocoa powder

1 tablespoon baking soda

1 tablespoon cinnamon

2¾ sticks unsalted butter, at room
 temperature

1½ cups sugar

1 teaspoon kosher salt

1 teaspoon vanilla extract

1 cup coarsely chopped bittersweet chocolate,
 melted

1 cup finely chopped bittersweet chocolate

Flaky salt, to finish (we like fleur de sel)

Preheat the oven to 325°F with racks in the
center and upper third of the oven. Line
2 baking sheets with parchment paper.

Combine the flour, cocoa powder, baking
soda, and cinnamon in medium bowl.

Using a stand mixer or an electric mixer
and a large bowl, beat the butter until soft
and fluffy. Add the sugar, salt, and vanilla
extract and beat for 1 minute. Slowly add the
dry ingredients, a little bit at a time, mixing
between each addition, until the dough is
crumbly. Add the melted chocolate while the
mixer is running. Add the finely chopped
chocolate and mix until just combined.

Roll the dough into four 2-inch-thick logs.
Wrap the logs in plastic and let chill for at
least an hour, until firm. You can store the
dough in the refrigerator for up to a week or
in the freezer for up to a month.

Slice the cookie dough into ¼-inch rounds and
arrange on the prepared baking sheets, spacing
them about 1 inch apart. Sprinkle with flaky
salt. Bake for 5 to 6 minutes, then switch the
positions of the pans in the oven and bake for
another 5 to 6 minutes.

Let cool on the baking sheets for 5 minutes
before serving.

EASY ALMOND CAKE WITH FRESH FRUIT

Makes one 8-inch round cake

A light and breezy dessert that's the perfect finish to any meal. You can also double the ingredients, use a larger pan, and bake for the same cooking time.

1 cup all-purpose flour

1¼ teaspoons baking powder

8 tablespoons (1 stick) unsalted butter

1¼ cup granulated sugar

2 large eggs

1½ teaspoons almond extract

1 cup mixed fresh fruit (such as raspberries, sliced peaches, mango, or pears)

Powdered sugar, to finish

Fresh whipped cream, berries, and chopped mint leaves, to serve (if desired)

Preheat the oven to 350°F. Grease and flour an 8-inch springform pan.

Combine the flour and baking powder in a medium bowl. Set aside.

Using an electric mixer and a large bowl, beat together the butter and sugar until pale and fluffy. Add the eggs one at a time and beat until combined. Add the almond extract.

Pour the flour mixture into the wet ingredients and mix with a wooden spoon until just incorporated. The batter should be thick. Spread it into the prepared pan. Arrange the fruit on top and bake for 55 to 60 minutes, until lightly browned and a tester inserted in the center comes out clean.

Let the cake cool on wire rack for 10 to 15 minutes, then remove the cake from the pan. Dust with powdered sugar, add a dollop of whipped cream, berries, and mint, if you like, and serve.

UNTIL NEXT TIME . . .

We really don't want to go, but it's time to for us to get back to work and for you to fly away from this cozy little nest to use and share what you have learned. Maybe it's introducing someone to a whole new look or just smiling and making eye contact with a stranger. We officially give you permission to go out and "queer eye" the world. It starts with you—now put your best foot forward!

ACKNOWLEDGMENTS

To the Fab Five for giving yourself to the show and to this endeavor—in the middle of a million other demands.

To David Collins and Michael Williams, who made regifting cool again by delivering a new version of Queer Eye as beloved as the original.

To Joel Chiodi and Rob Eric, whose creative vision, force of will, and ability to manifest got this book done.

To Amanda Englander, Ian Dingman, Mark McCauslin, Derek Gullino, Kate Tyler, Natasha Martin, Stephanie Davis, and Gabrielle Van Tassel at Clarkson Potter for their shared vision, determination, expertise, and stunning book-making.

To Margaret Riley King and Nir Caspi at WME for bringing everyone together, and to Haley Heidemann for her support.

To Monica Corcoran Harel, who adroitly captured five unique voices in one stellar manuscript.

To Denise Crew and her assistant, Alex Rhoades, for the gorgeous photography.

To Kwame Waters for his fabulous wardrobe-pulling and styling.

To Kristin Kent for hair and makeup.

To Beth Barden and her assistant, Melissa Poelling, for their food preparation and styling.

To Marnie Sauls for location support at Two Light.

To Netflix and ITV, our amazing partners in making this show.

ABOUT THE AUTHORS

BOBBY BERK'S rise to fame in the home design world didn't happen overnight. Originally hailing from Texas, Bobby had big dreams of the big city and moved to New York in 2003 with only a few dollars to his name and no job in sight. After working his way up in retail at Bed Bath & Beyond and Restoration Hardware to a Creative Director position at Portico Home + Spa, Berk decided it was time to create his own brand. Since 2006, Bobby Berk Home's retail division has consistently provided customers with a unique approach to modern design. Epitomizing hip, minimalist urban luxury, Berk's designs reflect a stylish and youthful spirit that perfectly fits any cool, relaxed lifestyle. In addition to his work on *Queer Eye*, Berk has also appeared as an expert on numerous television networks, including HGTV, Bravo, NBC, and CBS.

KARAMO BROWN is a TV personality most known for being the "culture expert" on *Queer Eye*, where he engages the subjects in important cultural conversations that help them get to the core of understanding themselves, so they can relate to the world better.

Karamo began his career in 2004 as a housemate on the hit MTV reality series *The Real World*, becoming the first openly gay African American in the history of reality TV. Shortly after the conclusion of *The Real World*, Karamo learned he had a nine-year-old biological child, whom he gained full custody of. He later left the spotlight to become a social worker and adopted his biological son's half-brother.

In February 2014, Karamo returned to television as a host and segment producer for *The OWN Show* on the Oprah Winfrey Network. He was subsequently hired as a host for *Huffington Post Live* and a Family Advocate contributor for HLN/CNN. In 2016, Karamo returned to reality television as a cast member on TV One's hit docuseries *#TheNext15*. The show documented Karamo's life after reality stardom, as he balanced being a single father with being a working professional. He is also the host of MTV's *Are You the One: Second Chances* and H2's *Breaking Mysterious*, which airs in the UK and Canada. Karamo is a guest contributor for *Access Hollywood Live* on NBC.

Karamo currently serves on the board for OutRight International, a leading international LGBTQI human rights organization dedicated to improving the lives of people who experience discrimination or abuse on the basis of their sexual orientation, sex characteristics, or gender identity worldwide. He also cofounded the nonprofit organization 6in10.org, which provides tailored mental health support for black gay and bisexual men in order to eradicate the 6 in 10 HIV statistic plaguing this community. In 2016, Karamo was invited by the Obama administration to work with the White House to create policy/legislation to support LGBTQ youth and their allies after school hours.

TAN FRANCE has been a successful fashion designer behind the scenes for more than fifteen years, and now has stepped into the spotlight of *Queer Eye* as the witty wardrobe wiz leading the charge in the fashion department. This experience is so much more than just new clothes to the British-born fashion advisor, however; it's about real-life issues, changes, and acceptance on all sides. The epitome of style and class, Tan is the creative mind behind such successful brands as the popular ladies' clothing lines Kingdom & State and Rachel Parcell, Inc. Prior to his personal success as a designer, he spent his summers working in his grandfather's denim factory while he secretly enrolled in fashion college.

ANTONI POROWSKI is the food and wine connoisseur on Netflix's reboot of the hit TV series *Queer Eye*. Growing up, Antoni was bitten by the culinary bug early, spending countless hours in the kitchen watching his mother cook. He discovered the worlds of Julia Child, Jacques Pépin, and Anthony Bourdain, and soon after began to teach himself how to cook. He immediately went to work in restaurants from Montreal to New York City, continuing to hone his craft and finding his place in the culinary world. This love of food and cooking led to him becoming the personal chef and protégé of original *Queer Eye* star Ted Allen. The relationship helped launch Antoni's career, and he became the personal chef to some of Manhattan's and Brooklyn's most prominent citizens.

JONATHAN VAN NESS is the *Queer Eye* grooming expert advisor. He grew up in Quincy, Illinois, before training as a hair stylist at the Aveda Institute in Minneapolis and then furthering his craft at Sally Hershberger in Los Angeles. Now he is a renowned hair stylist who works out of his own salon, Mojo Hair Studio in Los Angeles, and Arte in New York City. He has been the groomer at cast events for HBO shows *Game of Thrones* and *True Blood,* and since 2015 he has also been a stylist for E!'s *Fashion Police.* But he is probably best known as the host of the Emmy-nominated *Funny or Die* web series sensation *Gay of Thrones,* which millions tune into weekly for a hilarious

recap of *Game of Thrones. Gay of Thrones* has received stellar reviews from NBC, *Vulture, The Advocate,* and other news outlets.

Jonathan is a naturalist, and the underlying tenants of his grooming philosophy are self-love and self-acceptance, helping whomever he is working with to find the tools to feel like their best self.

DAVID COLLINS is a three-time Emmy Award–winning producer and co-owner of Scout Productions, a film and television company. He is the creator and executive producer of the Emmy-nominated *Queer Eye,* which launched unscripted programming on Netflix worldwide and is one of the most-buzzed-about shows of 2018. A critical and social media phenomenon, season 2 dropped in June.

Collins led on the original *Queer Eye for the Straight Guy,* which took home Emmys, two GLAAD awards, a Producers Guild of America "Producer of Year" award, among many other honors. Airing in over 120 countries with 19 original formats, *Queer Eye* was a vanguard contributor to the personal transformation reality boom of the past decade and a half. That series was created with his groundbreaking "Make Better" network model of storytelling, which immediately became the cornerstone of Bravo's network model and inspired scores of subsequent personal improvement reality programs.

Beyond *Queer Eye,* David has executive produced programs for Netflix, Bravo, ABC, NBC, IFC, A&E, VH1, and more. Recently the company expanded into short form for the NBCUniversal venture Bluprint's "Blank Wall Overhaul."

MICHAEL WILLIAMS is an Academy and Emmy Award–winning producer and co-owner of Scout Productions. Over

the course of his career, Michael has achieved considerable industry recognition, including an Oscar for producing Errol Morris's documentary *The Fog of War,* an Emmy for executive producing the barrier-breaking *Queer Eye for the Straight Guy,* and an Emmy for *OWN: Oprah Winfrey Network's Home Made Simple. Queer Eye,* in particular, also earned Michael the 2004 PGA Producer of the Year Award. He is currently executive producing the all-new *Queer Eye.*

ROB ERIC is an Emmy Award–winning television producer, film producer, and author who has developed and created media for screens large and small alongside producing partners Michael Williams and David Collins for more than ten years. He has produced for networks such as ABC, CBS, ABC Family, Bravo, HGTV, OWN, HBO, SONY, and Netflix, among others, with work ranging from interview and documentary series to makeover series to game shows. More recently, he has also developed scripted series with partners such as Sony Pictures Television, Left Bank Pictures, Flower Films, and Court Five Productions. Follow Rob on Instagram @roberic1.

MONICA CORCORAN HAREL is an award-winning journalist and author who writes about the culture of style for the *New York Times, ELLE, Marie Claire,* and *The Hollywood Reporter.* Her books include the *New York Times* bestseller *Living in Style* with celebrity stylist Rachel Zoe and *The Fashion File* with costume designer Janie Bryant. She also creates custom content and has worked with clients such as Morgan Stanley, Estée Lauder, and Lionsgate Films. She lives in Los Angeles with her husband and their daughter, Tess Darling.

CLARKSON POTTER is a trademark and POTTER
with colophon is a registered trademark of
Penguin Random House LLC.

Library of Congress
Cataloging-in-Publication Data
Names: Porowski, Antoni; France, Tan; Van Ness,
   Jonathan; Berk, Bobby; Brown, Karamo.
Title: Queer eye: love yourself, love your life
   / Antoni Porowski, Tan France, Jonathan Van
   Ness, Bobby Berk, and Karamo Brown; with
   Monica Corcoran Harel; photographs by Denise
   Crew and Gavin Bond.
Description: New York : Clarkson Potter, [2018]
Identifiers: LCCN 2018032937| ISBN 9781984823939
   (hardcover) | ISBN 9781984823946 (eISBN)
Subjects: LCSH: Self-acceptance. | Self-esteem.
   | Conduct of life.
Classification: LCC BF575.S37 P67 2018 | DDC
   155.2—dc23. LC record available at https://
   lccn.loc.gov/2018032937

ISBN 978-1-9848-2393-9
Ebook ISBN 978-1-9848-2394-6

Printed in the United States of America

Book and cover design by Ian Dingman.
Photographs by Denise Crew.
Cover photograph and photographs on page 2,
82, 99, 112, 125, 146, 163, 174, 187, 198, 213 by
Gavin Bond/Netflix.
Photograph on page 10 (bottom) courtesy of
David Collins.
Photographs on page 188 by Alex Rhoades.
Vintage photos courtesy of the Fab Five.
Illustrations by Paige Vickers.

10 9 8 7 6 5 4 3 2 1

First Edition